WORLD WAR II
IN
MEDINA COUNTY, OHIO

AT HOME & OVERSEAS

Eli R. Beachy

Charleston · London

THE
History
PRESS

Published by The History Press
Charleston, SC 29403
www.historypress.net

Copyright © 2014 by Eli R. Beachy
All rights reserved

First published 2014

Manufactured in the United States

ISBN 978.1.62619.298.0

Library of Congress CIP data applied for.

*In memory of the greatest mortal man who ever walked the face of the earth.
I never did get your whole story, but I did get theirs now.*

Thanks, Dad. In the end, we did all right.

CONTENTS

*The Greatest Generation of Medina * On a Sunday in December * Real Government Efficiency * Almost Forgotten * Producing a Victory * That Great Redhead * The Inside News of Invasion * The Million Dollar House of Medina * Fought by Men, Won by Women * Super Secret from Medina * In the Cause of Scrap * The Japanese Invasion of Medina * The Legend of the County Home * At the Expense of Fashion * Uncle Sam Wanted Him * With Pen and Paper * A Lady with a Past * Bad Advice Not Taken * A Financial Solution in the Past * A Thread to the Past * A Dangerous Eleven-Year-Old * Producing Victory One Spade at a Time * A Woman with One Great Regret * The Lost Tribe of Medina * An Amazing Idea Born in an Empty Field * An Ordinary Day at the Warehouse*

*A War Before the War * A Safe Assignment * The American Hero of Lodi * On the Isle of Saipan * Chasing the Weather * The Young Salt of Wadsworth * The Super's Son * The Prisoner Fenn * An Admiral a Long Way from Home * Fifty Times a Hero * The Birth of the EMT * Bad Time to Be First * The Feeding of the Masses * In the Matters*

PREFACE

This is a book that began to be formed more than forty years ago. It was a pleasant July morning in the early 1970s. The place was the Lawsonia Links Golf Course of Green Lake, Wisconsin. My father and I had been playing well at a couple over par in our round when we got to the sixteenth tee, catching up with a husband, wife and beautiful daughter who hadn't been having such a good day. Just for somebody to talk to, we all decided to finish out the round together.

As Dad pegged up his ball, our new friend introduced himself as Bud Woods of Wichita Falls, Texas. With that, my dad turned bone white, put a swing on the ball I didn't recognize and knocked his tee shot maybe fifty yards forward. As I walked past him to hit my own shot, Dad said, "Find out what that guy does."

An odd request in a round of golf, but I was a good son. I hit my driver well, made conversation with the daughter, who had little interest with me, and then reported back to Dad. This Bud Woods was a big brass with the United States Air Force at the base there in Texas. In an instant, Dad's color returned. He shrugged, pulled out a 2 iron, walked over to his ball and hit a screamer 250 yards down the fairway. What I didn't know was that one of those life moments was about to unfold.

I went ahead after everybody hit, not really thinking too much about what I had just seen, at least at the moment. My second shot was going to be pretty easy; a high-fade 4 iron should give me a chance for bird, and I might pick up a shot or two. As I considered the possibilities and began my setup,

Dad walked up. Just as I was about to draw back, I managed to ask what that topped shot he'd hit was all about.

"I worked for a Bud Woods at the end of the war," Dad said with a somewhat indifferent shrug. "Only man ever authorized to carry a side arm at all times."

"Oh yeah? Why was that?"

"He was the U.S. Army hangman."

They're still looking for my golf ball to this day in the Wisconsin woods. I have no idea where the Titleist 2 with a penciled X under each T might have gone—my mind was somewhat distracted by the revelation that had just been laid on me. I had known that Dad was in the service in World War II and that he had been a combat engineer in Europe, but not much else when it came to facts. Come to find out I didn't know the man I loved with all my heart at all. More importantly, I wasn't going to find out.

Like the overwhelming majority of true combat veterans, Dad rarely spoke of his time in World War II. He would tell a funny story now and then, but he wasn't the guy who won the war. He, like so many others, lived by the adage that "You weren't there; you wouldn't understand." Instead of reporting, he was going to spend the next forty years giving me snippets.

A word here and a reference there, and I would return to my research texts, trying to put another piece into the giant puzzle that was his military career. I eventually got a lot of it before Dad died ten years ago, but not all. Not even half, to be honest. Just enough to make an interesting read, but that wasn't what he wanted. Not Dad.

The Bronze Star recipient for his action at the Stavelot fuel dump, the construction foreman for the U.S. Army hangman and the guy they called "Stinky" never wanted it to be about him. It was always about the other guys, guys who he said really did something. Other stories that should be told, whether anybody would ever understand them or not.

So, for more than forty years, I looked, exploring one topic and then another in the mystifying subject we labeled World War II. The books, the maps, the artifacts and the vets—each was a source for one more layer of comprehension. Forty years plus of trying to figure out what to do with it all.

Then I found Medina County, Ohio.

ACKNOWLEDGEMENTS

My B.W., who loves her research. Frank and Marilyn Ehrman, whose kitchen table was the source of inspiration. George Hudnutt, the only publisher who gave me a chance to spread the story. You each will never know how much you meant to make this real. "Thank you" isn't enough, but I do not know what is.

Introduction

It's an easy place to miss, this geographic entity called Medina County, Ohio. Within its 450 square miles, there is little to attract the average traveler. The great amusement park is long gone, and there are no fantastic festivals nor any natural wonders. All that is left is what has been a part of Medina County for the last two thousand years: some most amazing people.

The first known inhabitants had towns and commerce well established in this area a thousand years before Columbus sailed for a New World. They were the Hopewell cultures, but today a single mound and a few shattered artifacts are all that remain to mark their existence. The Woodlands tribes that followed left little more, nor did the first Europeans, the French and English trappers. Civilization was coming in each passing year but was not going to be recorded until 1832.

It was that year when the *Medina County Gazette* first began publication, covering all the local news fit to print and all the editorial comment anybody cared to read. There were calves birthed and picnics out at a lake called Chippewa to be reported, along with what last week's weather had been. As time went by and subscribers grew, the paper became the mouthpiece for all right-thinking Americans, just as long as they voted the straight Republican ticket.

The *Gazette* supported Fremont before it knew Abe was the man. There was no finer president than Grant, unless it was Hayes or maybe Garfield. Throughout the nineteenth century, the paper toted the Grand Old Party's banner and trumpeted the returning veterans of that great Civil War. The only national news that needed reporting was that which possibly could affect the locals. It truly was the center of the world, this Medina County, Ohio, at least according to one press—a tradition that continued on long after the horse had been replaced by horsepower and the world went to war once and then again. All the time, it was always about the people we all knew.

So it was during World War II, the news of great battles found on the airways of the radio or in some big-city paper. For the *Gazette*, it was always, each and every edition, about the hometown men and women who were answering the call. Always about the bond drive that raised so much or the scrap drive that went so well. It was a newspaper for the people and about the people who called Medina County home. People who should have been enshrined long before now.

Nearly 3,000 young men and women left Medina County to serve their nation in the armed services; 150 never came home, 14 of them not found to this day. They were in North Africa and the Canal, Anzio and the Bulge, doing whatever asked of them. No Congressional Medal of Honor recipients, just thousands of brave men and women trying to do as well as the folks back home.

As the soldiers, sailors and Marines went off to battle, those behind went to work. They did their jobs, they accepted rationing, they collected scrap and they bought war bonds by the millions, all in the name of preserving the American way of life. There was no glory, no medals and very little recognition, but there was none expected. It was all about duty at home and abroad until that war could be won. Fairly won, at horrible cost, all so the greatest collection of humanity in American history could quietly fade into the background of our way of life.

There was no chest-thumping, no glorious attempts at self-promotion from those who had been to World War II. They simply came home and went about their business, creating a community and an economy that thrived for years, even as the inevitable would come calling—that those who had faded into the background would slowly, surely, begin fading away to eternity.

So it is today, the overwhelming majority of those who actually were eyewitnesses to the history of World War II have passed away. Few remain, but perhaps that is just as well. The world is not what they left when they went off to service, and it is certainly not what they came back to build. Instead of initiative, it is now entitlement; instead of duty, it has become self. To the kid who wintered in a foxhole at the Bulge, it could well be a world he would never recognize.

He knew that he was smarter than a fifth grader. He knew if he couldn't sing or dance; there was no reason to make a fool out of himself trying in public. His personal life was no soap opera for a talk show. There were no questions he needed a pseudo-psychologist to answer save one—he never will figure out when the rest of us finally realize that history is nothing but the past tense of the present.

Holding the image of the "Greatest Generation" up for inspection is not holding a mirror to our world today. There is, however, the great life lesson to be found somewhere in their past. That the ordinary Joe and Jane were extraordinary human beings when their nation called. So extraordinary that they must not ever be forgotten, no matter how ordinary they might have wanted to be.

So it was that this project began, a series of newspaper columns in that one paper that had always made it about the individual, the *Medina County Gazette*. Every Thursday, they decorate the editorial page, 750 words at a time, trying to capture some of the greatness that once was so common in a most ordinary community.

The articles that appear here are in their essentially original submission form. I have always been well aware that a Distinguished Scholar of History should be capitalized and that a jeep used in World War II should not. I do not write single-sentence paragraphs, nor do I care if that is the current style of journalism. I have also used "I" five more times than should be done.

It's not about us. It's all about them and the America they made, and this book shows just some of the ways they, the Greatest, did just that.

Part I

HOME

THE GREATEST GENERATION OF MEDINA

April 5, 2012

It is the definition of insanity to repeat behavior over and over again while expecting a different outcome. Those actions are also a reasonable review of American history. Ever since the signing of the Declaration of Independence, we of this nation have continually replayed events gone wrong with the total belief that it was about to turn out right. Should there be any doubt, consider the life and times of one hundred years ago.

A Gilded Age had come and gone as the calendar turned to 1912, with the country trying to reinvent itself in its wake. A presidential election was gearing up, progressive versus arch-conservative factions ready to solicit votes as they slung mud with gusto. Crime was up in cities and rural areas, educational achievement was down and the old soldiers who defined a nation were dying out every single day.

With every printing in newspapers across the country, lip service was paid to the ancient warriors of Blue or Gray through the obituary column—a name printed, the vital dates of birth and then death, mention of service in the war and perhaps a unit designation as well. Occasionally, there might even be a brief sentence of some notable battle survived. It was all just in passing, news of the day being so much more important, or so we thought.

In 1930, they played war in their fathers' old uniforms, and it was all a game. Twelve years later, the game was played in hell, but they both would survive Bataan. *Sharon Beachy Collection.*

The old veterans no longer marched in the Memorial Day parades of 1912; that was left to the young bucks who had recently battled Spain. The troopers of the Union army rode in carriages or those newfangled automobiles. They carried canes, their white hair blowing in the wind as their waves became more and more feeble. The smoky fields of Gettysburg or Pittsburg Landing were fading memories, stories nobody wanted to hear any more. Occasionally, there would be a civic drive to erect another statue, but it didn't really matter. Great wars were over, happy days were sure to come again and the old veterans just kept slipping away as their history would pass with them.

So it is today in this world sometimes gone crazy from the life that grew out of the remnants of World War II. An election is coming, crime is up, standards are down and we turn to the obituary page and note American flags by life descriptions. With each passing day, more of the veterans of that conflict are no more. Each day, their stories escape, their history almost lost. A history that little old Medina County was so involved in that it almost is beyond belief.

A Medina County boy died at Pearl Harbor, but another former resident was already involved in the shooting war in Africa at the time. The good citizens of the area panicked in December 1941, totally convinced of imminent invasion, while hundreds of young men showed up to enlistment offices and draft boards. Young men who would be eventually at the Bulge or a place called Guadalcanal. Courageous American heroes who understood very quickly what real wars were all about.

Off to Parris or Pendleton they went, while their classmates headed to Bowie or Jackson and a neighbor reported to Great Lakes. Into every branch of service locals came, off to do their duty and save a nation and a world under attack. They looked so fine in their new uniforms, and they wrote home, telling the folks how well things were going as a drill instructor screamed in their ear. As they shipped out from Basic, they were still such kids, all about to grow up fast.

It happened at the Canal or maybe Tarawa. For some, it was North Africa or in the bomb bay of a B-17. For others, it was at Remagen or Anzio, or a nursing station in bocage country. For one, it was when he walked through the front gates of a place called Buchenwald, another with the last calculation of an equation that completed the Manhattan Project. Wherever it was, Medina County kids were there, turning into men and women. Men and women who must be immortal.

Forever they will be the handsome young fellows in dress blues or pinks, ordinary children who became adults in hell. We must remember them for what they once did. At least one mistake of the past won't be repeated for a while. Their stories will not die one week at a time. They are the Greatest Generation from right here in little old Medina County, USA.

ON A SUNDAY IN DECEMBER

April 12, 2012

The sermons had run late that day, the second Sunday of Advent bringing out the Christmas spirit in pulpits around town. By the time the good ladies of the Episcopal or Methodist faith got home, the pot roasts and ham were almost burned. The food survived, though, more than good enough to satisfy the family on a lazy day. Dinner was a little late, the radio was on for background noise and then the world stopped. It was December 7, 1941, in Medina, Ohio.

It was just after 2:30 p.m. when nationally based broadcasts began to break into programming with newsflashes. It was all off-the-wire service, truly transmitted by wire via the telegraph, the reports of an attack on the naval base at Pearl Harbor. Not everyone in Medina County listened to national broadcasts on a Sunday afternoon however. Not all heard, and few understood at first. Pearl was just something somewhere out in the Pacific. By five o'clock, that had changed. The entire county now knew and began to comprehend. It was time to mobilize to action.

Officially, war was not declared on the Empire of Japan until the next day, December 8. It took an appeal from the president of the United States and an act of Congress for that conflict to begin. Two days later, on the tenth, the German government made it easier for the nation, declaring war on the United States for reasons that remain to this day somewhat perplexing. It didn't matter to the good people of Medina; they had already started to create their own response, and it was called Civil Defense.

Civil Defense, keeping the homefront safe whether it needed it or not. Even if the Germans never did get around to bombing northern Ohio, we were ready. *Sharon Beachy Collection.*

Reverend Dr. John Quinton was one of the pastors who had gone on a bit long that Sunday, but he was a man who always wanted to cover all the bases all the time. That's why he'd been appointed executive director of the Medina County Civilian Defense program some months before December 7, when war truly appeared inevitable. A man of planning and then action, the parish priest knew his first move. It was time to call in the veterans.

Within forty-eight hours of the Pearl Harbor attack, companies of Home Guards were being organized in Medina. The American Legion would provide the nucleus in one unit, the doughboys still able to turn out in the defense of a nation.

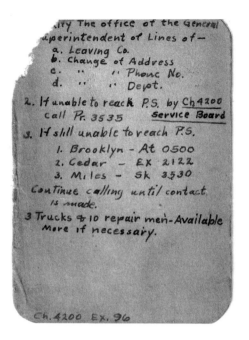

Top-secret instructions to save the Cleveland power grid when the Germans bombed the city. Keep calling until somebody answers. *Sharon Beachy Collection.*

From the citizens would come two more companies in support. When local police and sheriff's offices could no longer handle emergencies to come, they would be ready to step in and restore order. Having dealt with land invasion, Reverend Quinton turned his attention to the real threat to America: the attack from the air.

Over the next six months, one of the most detailed, complex and totally effective systems of air defense was organized in Medina County. More than one hundred volunteers turned out to form an intricate system of interlocking zones of observation over the area. There were training classes twice a week and even a visit from English firemen who had fought the fires of the London Blitz to motivate the community. There were uniforms, armbands and a job well done by one and all. Not once did the Germans bomb Medina.

Of course, one other detail might have had something to do with the spotless record of the Medina Civil Defense force. At the time of America's intervention in World War II, the most effective bomber in Hitler's arsenal was the JU-88—the merchant of death with a sixty-five-foot wingspan, six machine guns and a three-ton capacity. To bomb Medina, the ship would have to call a truce before it left Berlin, refuel in Scotland, Iceland and Nova Scotia and then pick up a payload of bombs in Toronto to reach the target, temporarily ending the truce before calling it again and then reversing the process to get home. It was a small detail but familiar all the same. After all, we are Americans.

Given a national emergency, the citizens of this country traditionally first impersonate headless chickens in reaction. Lasting from one day to six months, that irrationality is then replaced by resolve and finally by the achievement of the objective. So it was for America in 1941, everybody overreacting in every corner of the nation. In the end, it would be our finest hour. As 1941 came to a close, it was time for an ancient law to step up. It's the forgotten essential we called "the Draft," and it was about to come to every household in America.

REAL GOVERNMENT EFFICIENCY

April 19, 2012

It was born in Dixie during the Civil War, and it died when military service was no longer considered a necessity for American boys. Officially called the Selective Training and Service Act, it was always known as "the Draft," the last option of drawing young men into military service of the United States. Boards, cards and classifications are almost forgotten now—more American life gone by.

The Draft certainly had not started nor ended in high esteem among American people in different times. Its inception created riots, as did its death throes. In 1863, it was racial, with Irish residents rising up against the new competition in the workplace: the black man and woman. By the late 1960s and into the '70s, it was a social upheaval that would alter a nation. For late 1941, though, the Draft was the only way to make sense out of desperate need.

Opposite, bottom: Whether already in uniform or not, there would always be another government form to be filled out. *Diane Bumba Collection.*

DUPLICATE 1/21/46 – HONORABLE DISCHARGE
REGISTRATION CERTIFICATE
This is to certify that in accordance with the
Selective Service Proclamation of the President of the United States

ROBERT LEE COTTON
(First name)   (Middle name)   (Last name)
255 East Broad St. Elyria, Ohio
(Place of residence)
(This will be identical with line 2 of the Registration Card)

has been duly registered this 16 day of October, 19 40

-S-Mary B. McGuirs- Elyria,
(Signature of registrar)
Registrar for Local Board 3 Lorain Ohio
(Number)   (City or county)   (State)

THE LAW REQUIRES YOU TO HAVE THIS CARD IN YOUR
PERSONAL POSSESSION AT ALL TIMES
D. S. S. Form 2   16—21631
(Revised 6/9/41)

A long-forgotten essential in every young man's wallet until the early 1970s: the Draft Card. *Diane Bumba Collection.*

OPA Form R-570
Form Approved
Budget Bureau No. 08-R437

UNITED STATES OF AMERICA
OFFICE OF PRICE ADMINISTRATION

APPLICATION FOR RENEWAL OF
BASIC MILEAGE RATION
"A" or "D" Book

PART A
(See Instructions on other side)

NAME OF REGISTERED OWNER: (PRINT OR TYPE)
Willard J. DeWitt
COMPLETE ADDRESS OF REGISTERED OWNER:
14720 Detroit Ave
Lakewood, Ohio
RATION BOOK TO BE SENT TO: (CHECK ONE)
☑ REGISTERED OWNER (NAMED ABOVE)
☐ APPLICANT (NAMED BELOW)
APPLICANT'S NAME: (IF SAME AS OWNER WRITE "SAME")
Same
APPLICANT'S COMPLETE ADDRESS:

1. Was the enclosed back cover taken from the basic ration book issued for the vehicle described on this application? YES ☑ NO ☐
2. Is this vehicle in use and operating under currently valid license plates? YES ☑ NO ☐

Applicant must sign this Part A and must fill in all spaces in heavy border on both parts A and B.

I CERTIFY that all statements and answers made in this application are true and correct to the best of my knowledge and belief.

Signature Willard J. DeWitt
Date

	IDENTIFICATION OF VEHICLE	SERIAL NUMBERS OF TIRES LAST INSPECTED	
	VEHICLE LICENSE NO.: JL-463		
BOARD ACTION	STATE OF REGISTRATION: Ohio		Be sure to enter in the lower left-hand box on Part B the name and address to which the new Ration Book and Tire Inspection Record are to be sent.
Serial Number of Ration Book Issued	YEAR MODEL: 1936		
Issued	MAKE: Packard		
By Date	BODY TYPE: Sedan		

PART B
UNITED STATES OF AMERICA—OFFICE OF PRICE ADMINISTRATION
TIRE INSPECTION RECORD
Board certifies below that serial numbers shown are same as those registered with it.

Board Number	IDENTIFICATION OF VEHICLE	SERIAL NUMBERS OF TIRES LAST INSPECTED	1ST INSPECTION (REQUIRED SERVICE (IF NONE, WRITE "NONE"))
	VEHICLE LICENSE NO.: JL-463		
	STATE OF REGISTRATION: Ohio		None
(COUNTY) (STATE)	YEAR MODEL: 1936		
	MAKE: Packard		
By Date	BODY TYPE: Sedan		

		INSPECTION STATION NUMBER	APPOINTED BY WAR PRICE AND RATION BOARD		
A book holder, inspection every 6 months.	Inspector will not sign until required repair has been done.		NUMBER	COUNTY	STATE
B book holder, inspection every 4 months.					
C book holder, inspection every 3 months.					

		DATE:	INSPECTOR'S SIGNATURE:

RETURN TO:
Name Willard J. DeWitt
No. and Street 14720 Detroit Ave.
City and State Lakewood, Ohio.

	MILEAGE RATION BOOKS ISSUED		
	CLASS	SERIAL NUMBER	DATE

OPA Form R-570
Form Approved
Budget Bureau No. 08-R437

16—34287-1

With the attack on Pearl Harbor and then the Germans' declaration of war on the United States, dozens of Medina boys rushed to enroll in the military. It wasn't about job training or housing loans; it was anger and indignation at a foreign government or two that made them want, made them beg, to serve their Uncle Sam any way possible. Unlike during the Civil War or the Vietnam era, the Draft was not about forcing bodies into uniforms. At the start of World War II, it became all about saving the military a whole lot of time.

An enlistment office in December 1941 was not the science it is today. Many were little more than pamphlet centers, not equipped for much in the way of examinations of potential candidates. The war spurred on facilities unprepared for a rush, even though the United States required one year of

Later, it would become a postcard, but the sentiment was the same: greetings. It was time to serve where Uncle Sam sent you. *Diane Bumba Collection.*

military service from every young man. The government was about to establish that it can be efficient, and the Draft would prove to be the perfect funnel for men ready to do anything in the name of a nation.

Operating as Selective Service Boards, local appointees assembled eligible young men and sent them to Cleveland for physical examination. The potential recruits were classified into one of thirteen categories and returned, with the board notified of status. As quotas for the service were announced, the enlistees were called into duty by classification and given orders to report for basic training. It was a quick process that made great reading.

Just five days after the attack on Pearl Harbor, fifty-nine young men of Medina County were sent north for physicals, the news reported in the *Gazette*. So, too, was the fact that Elmo McVicker, once rejected on physical grounds, had now been accepted into the service. Personal privacy was not a high priority in the media at the outbreak of the war. Enlistee McVicker was 1-A, his pastor a 4-D and neighbor employed with the electric company a 2-A, all listed in the daily paper. It was a situation that got immediate government attention.

Long before the Patriot Act, the United States had some sense of national security. It was only weeks into the war when the directive came to Selective Service offices to cease and desist publishing details regarding the registration of enlistees as a military secret. German and Japanese agents were believed to be able to read, the astute observer from a belligerent nation therefore able to determine American troop level. Perhaps, too, the government was afraid the enemy might find out about the Hruska family and think they had a chance.

For all the patriotic fervor, not everyone supported America's war. In Hinckley, it was the Hruskas, two brothers who found their belief in the faith called Jehovah's Witness stronger than their obligation to register for the Draft and become 4-F. They would be arrested by the Federal Bureau of Investigation (FBI), tried and convicted, serving two years for the offense. For them, it was a matter of belief, but another Medina County boy was finding another kind of prison at the exact same moment, all for being at the wrong place at the wrong time.

Bobby Ring of Litchfield didn't have to worry about Selective Service and physicals in Cleveland. He never ducked the Draft, having enlisted in the United States Army in 1940. He dodged Japanese bullets in the Philippines instead. At least, right up until he was captured and started off on what became known as the Bataan Death March. Many were about to visit the ultimate hell on earth to find one of the war's greatest injustices.

ALMOST FORGOTTEN

April 26, 2012

It is the United States Department of Justice Criminal Division Human Rights and Special Prosecution Section. For thirty-three years, it has been given the charge to track down Nazi war criminals who have entered the United States. Having so identified, it maintains the authority to deport with the expectation, if not demand, of full prosecution by whatever country accepts the detained. The office of thirty government employees has been successful 107 times over the thirty-three years, bound by its charge and the restrictions limiting its work to Nazis within the borders of this country. How sad that it never got the chance to look for Mr. Sueymoto.

Litchfield's Bob Ring knew Private Sueymoto and a lot more like him. They became acquainted on April 9, 1942, when the American forces holding out in the Philippines finally surrendered to the Japanese. More than seventy-five thousand Americans were suddenly thrown into captivity, the largest surrender of a United States military force in history. It was the beginning of a cultural clash that was nothing but criminal.

In the Japanese military thinking of the time, it was the soldier's duty to die in the name of his cause, to give up life for the good of the emperor. To surrender to an enemy was an act of cowardice, an act of the greatest shame. By capitulating, the American soldiers in the Philippines had surrendered more than their weapons; they had given up their right to equality. They were nothing more than animals, beasts to be used, nothing more and usually much, much less.

Subsequent apologists have attempted to justify the Japanese actions as an army overwhelmed by the number of prisoners suddenly thrust on it. Attempting to deal in the world of political correctness, they propose the theory that it was a lack of logistics, not intent, that created the situation about to unfold. Historical facts present another picture—that it was premeditated murder that began with a thing forever known as the Bataan Death March.

Bob Ring was there, one of the tens of thousands of prisoners forced into a line and then moved forward. To stop without orders was to die by either bayonet or decapitation from a saber, the Japanese being unwilling to waste a bullet on animals. A man heeded the call of nature as he walked, the only food and drink not much more than a cup of rice and a few swallows of water. For sixty miles they marched, from Mariveles to San Fernando, and then they were packed into trucks for the ride to the prison known as Camp O'Donnell. All under the most watchful eye of Private Sueymoto and his associates.

There is no evidence that Private Sueymoto was anything but a proper soldier by American standards. Historians who would prefer the situation go away have identified extremely isolated moments of Japanese kindness during the march. There is also no evidence that Sueymoto was not the typical Japanese guard who had no qualms about stabbing a prisoner who stumbled, murder in the name of orders. About ten thousand would die in the week it took to walk those sixty miles. Bob Ring survived, one of the unlucky ones.

For more than two years, hell opened its jaws in the savage conditions of Camp O'Donnell until finally, on November 10, 1944, Robert V. Ring died from malaria, cholera, dysentery and abuse. Private Sueymoto watched from the guard tower as his body was carried away. The Americans eventually would return, but for thousands like Bob Ring, it was too late. They are still there, interred in unmarked graves around what once was a prison camp.

There would be a trial after the surrender, an official War Crimes Commission investigating the situation. A Japanese commander would be executed for war crimes, but there wasn't time or money to track down the guards who found murder second nature. There wouldn't have even been a hunt for the Nazis involved in the Holocaust without intense lobbying by the Department of Justice. In a short time, the trials ended, and life went on with one final injustice yet to play out.

Far easier it was for a war-weary America to let some things go and develop a trading partner in those postwar years. Sixty years later, justice continued to chase Nazi war criminals, Mr. Sueymoto died quietly in his Tokyo apartment surrounded by his loving family—just another war veteran—and almost nobody knew who Bobby Ring was, even in his hometown.

PRODUCING A VICTORY

May 10, 2012

It's just a very large, abandoned building today, perhaps the first symbol of the economic recession that finally came to Medina. An eyesore now, windows broken, grass grown up, the old Permold plant on State Route 18 is standing silent, unwilling to give up its secrets with just a glance. Once

They were the Rosies, the wives and sweethearts who stayed home to make industry work and pump up their men's morale any way they could. *Sharon Beachy Collection.*

upon a time, though, this was the queen of all business in the area. Once upon a time, this is where they saved a nation.

The smoke had barely cleared from Pearl Harbor when the U.S. Navy came calling to Permold. It wasn't a request; it was an emergency. One U.S. fleet was decimated, and all ships were vulnerable. A war was on. The United States Navy had to be rebuilt and reorganized in hours, not days. The workers of Medina couldn't create the next strategy that would replace outdated war by battleship, but they could help build the ships that would restore the fleet. It was a duty that Permold was ready, willing and able to perform.

The factory was almost perfect for production even before December 7, 1941. The equipment was all in place, in ready working order. There was an expertise in the labor to deal with this new miracle metal, aluminum. The trains, the only way to move goods before the advent of Kenworth and Freightliner, ran a spur right beside the plant. Secure from coastal attack, this was the ideal place to form navy castings, with one exception: there wasn't anybody to work there.

Between the patriotic fervor that drew young men into the service and the needs of the navy, the Permold factory was overextended almost immediately in terms of a labor force. The needs of a military rebuilding were going to require a 24/7 operation in little old Medina, a situation we only dream of today. For the executives at Permold, the problem was actually a simple solution. It was just a matter of looking down Dixie way.

Out of the hills of Kentucky the new workers would come, with word of mouth and rumor drawing laborers in search of a life, any life, outside of the hard times in Appalachia. By car and bus they came, their possessions packed in a suitcase or two, looking for a new life and money. They would find both, but it would take a couple of months to resolve one other issue: the new war workers had nowhere to live.

Cosmopolitan Medina was not exactly a hotbed of temporary housing at the start of World War II. Rooms to rent were few, with the labor pool growing by the hour. Again, to Permold, the solution was simple, and the result was a permanent addition to the Medina landscape. Today it's called the Lincoln Crossing Apartments on Marks Road, but in 1942, it was truly temporary, nothing more than a trailer park. Permanent structures were a year away, a year the labor force of Permold put to record use.

The year 1942 had just begun when the announcement came from the Department of the Navy in Washington. Of all the industries in the country, Medina's Permold was one of the first four chosen for excellence in production. In the name of the war effort, public morale and continued progress, the brass were coming to Medina the next month. With them was coming a most holy grail.

It was known as the E Flag, a red-and-blue pennant displaying a gold *E* within a golden wreath. Officially called the Navy Production Award, later changed to the Army-Navy Production Award, the banner represented the recognition of the highest quality of production in the name of the war effort and was a civilian equivalent of the Congressional Medal of Honor. It was a flag only awarded to the best for their best effort, an award that merited great celebration. Seventy years later, and it is an award long forgotten in many ways.

Throughout the duration of World War II, Permold flew its award, striving every

They gave medals on the battlefield for courageous dedication. At home, the E Flag was the prize of heroes. *Diane Bumba Collection.*

day for even greater quality, even greater production, but wars do not last forever. With the Japanese surrender, the need for aluminum castings, as made on State Route 18, ceased. Workers went off to other endeavors, and slowly the Permold empire began to collapse. By 2014, there is nothing left but an empty building. Nothing remains of the greatness—not even a flag. Perhaps it is in a box, buried in a closet or an attic somewhere, waiting to be found. The highest honor, deserving so much more, hiding somewhere waiting to be found.

That Great Redhead

May 17, 2012

They loved redheads once upon a time in Medina County, or at least one who wasn't named Lucy. According to the local lore, anybody who met County Health Nurse Helen Smathers and didn't fall in love must have been a candidate for the insane asylum. The carrot-topped bundle of energy won the hearts and minds of everyone she met in a unanimous opinion. Given the nature of the job in 1941, she'd managed to meet just about everybody.

In a school one day and sitting at a farmer's kitchen table the next, Miss Smathers combined the advent of modern medicine with the last gasps of ancient administration. For every shot given, there were three pages of paperwork to be filled out and then filed by hand. She fought measles epidemics and outbreaks of chickenpox seven days a week, her radiant beauty drying many the tear of fear. It was a job she loved and one that loved her, but there was an even greater love for the sweetheart of Medina. One she ran to come December 7, 1941, the United States of America.

It goes with the nursing profession—that occupation all about duty, not convenience or exploiting financial gain. That's the way it was in 1941 and continues on to this day. For Helen Smathers, that duty to the needs of a nation was far greater than all the assistance she could render little old Medina County. In a perfect world, she would have stayed forever, but the Japanese had made it a most imperfect time. With a fond farewell and a promise to stay in touch, the Medina County nurse was off to save the world. She never expected that it would become an adventure right out of a romance novel.

Within a few weeks of Pearl Harbor, County Health Nurse Helen was Lieutenant Smathers, sailing into Manila Bay as part of an army relief mission. Instead of chickenpox and mumps, it was dysentery and cholera to be treated, on a peninsula called Bataan. Instead of broken bones, it was bullet wounds, but the hours remained the same. It was twenty-four hours a day of duty. The Japanese were coming and weren't going to be stopped.

American strategy in the Philippines had been based on fighting a delaying action until relief forces could be mobilized from the United States. Unfortunately for the War Department in Washington, the Japanese hadn't read that strategy manual, preferring a relentless assault. In short order, the American defensive action became a withdrawal that bordered on a rout. The islands were lost; all that was left was to remove as many as possible to Australia no matter how much a nurse might have objected.

It is unclear if Lieutenant Smathers was on the last boat from Bataan. For certain, she left in the last hours of freedom, protesting all the way down the dock, onto the boat and to Australia. It was duty. Critical care nursing was far more important in her mind than her own safety, even as bullets flew around her. For the army, it was another matter, even beyond the preventing of a beautiful woman from falling into enemy hands. They were out to make Helen Smathers a celebrity.

Despite her objections, the noble nurse with the unforgettable looks had little time for administering injections Down Under. The army made her a fashion model for new uniforms, the public face of the noble nurses who had faced combat in the name of mercy. It was never Helen Smathers's intention to be anything but a nurse, but it was an order all the same. Within a month, her photograph was in all the dailies across America in the name of morale. She was a most valuable asset to the war effort but was about to become even more valuable to a reporter named Martin.

She mentioned this Martin in passing in a letter back to friends in Medina a few months later and then again the next month. Helen Smathers was an outstanding nurse but even better at keeping secrets, at least when it came to the man of her dreams. Within a few more months, she and Martin were headed back to Washington, she serving out the war in administrative duties and public appearances, waiting patiently for new husband Martin to come home each evening.

Husband Martin Agronski, lead reporter for NBC Radio News for the next thirty years, the one generals, presidents and everyone else listened to all across the nation.

THE INSIDE NEWS OF INVASION

June 7, 2012

It's a weighty responsibility to be blessed with sudden and complete understanding. It was a mantle the venerable war analyst Spencer Irwin accepted gladly, though, as the calendar turned to 1944. As the rest of the world waited and wondered, Irwin already had the answer to the ages. He knew exactly where the Allies were going to invade Fortress Europe and a very good idea of when. Being the true American that he was, Mr. Irwin felt that he had an obligation to tell anybody who might listen.

As it so happened, Medina County was the first stop of the sage's world tour that last Saturday of January in 1944. In the auditorium of the high school, the County Teacher's Association had come together, the traditional boring monthly meeting suddenly an event all wanted to attend. They waited with bated breath for the great man to arrive, every teacher armed with notebook and pencil, ready to learn. Of all places on earth, it would be here that was about to be first to know the greatest military secret in the history of world.

For eighteen months, German agents from Lisbon to Stockholm had tried to unlock the mystery without success. Countless hours had been spent by German high commands of the land, sea and air for the same purpose, with the same result. The world knew that an invasion was coming, but it could be anywhere from Palestine to Norway and all points in between. These Allies were learning the art of secrecy after all.

In theory, constitutional governments based on individual liberties, such as the United Kingdom and the United States, should be the least likely to veil military operations from public view. Logically, that is frightening—that a first-term congressman has the right to monitor the actions of a four-star general and then the duty to report his findings to the local newspaper. It is the framework of our governments, though, weighing heavily on that forgotten aspect known as individual responsibility. Within that framework of openness, the United States military worked quite well. It would just plain lie about it.

By the time war analyst Spencer Irwin started to set up his charts and maps that Saturday in Medina, most of the world had heard that the invasion that would be eventually known as Overload was headed to the Pas-de-Calais of France. Those truly in the know already understood that it would be Patton's attack, a massive assault supported by armor, giving the Germans a dose of the American blitzkrieg. With much delight that bordered on glee, Irwin was proud to announce to the local teachers that nothing could be further from the truth. Unfortunately for the teachers, so was Irwin.

For two hours, the educators listened with quiet admiration to the stupidest theory of invasion ever laid before public review. The brilliant mind had figured out that it was not southern France, not Calais, not Greece and not Holland but in fact directly into Germany the invasion would go. Even though the Nazis might not expect landing craft at the mouth of the Elbe, Spencer Irwin did, despite a few small details that might slow the attack. Details like the German navy, air force and army all headquartered near one another. That and a thousand other facts. At least it was entertaining for a couple of hours.

Spencer Irwin is not known to have ever given his presentation again. There didn't seem to be much call for any more harebrained thinking. He went back to his job as a war analyst for that bastion of the truth the *Cleveland Plain Dealer*, and the teachers went back to their classrooms that next Monday. A few thousand miles away, four kids set back to their work as well.

For Charlie Young, it was another day stowing gear around the galley, making space for what was to come. One more time Bob Shane led his platoon down the ropes into what the army called a landing craft. For Bob Johnson and Carl Fallor, it was trying not to get sick as they practiced sprinting to a beachhead through seawater. Four kids busy, too busy to worry too much what a crackpot reporter might think. Too busy hoping for just one thing.

On June 7, 1944, they got it. They'd survived D-Day, alive and well to fight again. Fight, just as long as the folk back home kept understanding how much they themselves were giving to the cause of a total victory.

THE MILLION DOLLAR HOUSE OF MEDINA

June 14, 2012

It is the Million Dollar House of Medina, but nobody ever lived in it. Nothing more than a shack that is still standing today after seventy years, it once was the center of a financial universe—a most important building and an even more important concept that would bring Hollywood to Medina just to see it and the people who made it happen. Now we just rush past it as we go by Medina Hospital. It is the War Bond Office, and we have completely forgotten how great we once were, right here in Medina County, USA.

The simple white structure was constructed of wood and built on the three basic American principles of commerce: war is good business, war is expensive business and any expensive business is best funded by other people's money. Defense contractors would get rich in World War II as the government spent more money in four years than it had in the previous century and a half. A Democrat administration came up with a creative income plan that went beyond demanding higher taxes. It was going to let Americans ballot with their wallets.

Being a republic, not a democracy, American citizens do not vote for war. That is a job for representatives and senators. Having been so voted, that in no way ensures the support of the constituent back home. As the opposition to intervention stood at 90 percent of the electorate in the summer of 1941, it seemed unlikely the administration's plan on selling bonds to finance a militarizing nation was particularly feasible. On the morning of December 8, 1941, it became a matter of economic brilliance.

Suddenly every American supported war and was motivated to do anything and everything possible to confirm a love of nation. The kids went to enlist, and the bankers remembered that bond thing that had come around the summer before. A ten-year note, paying 2.9 percent, not a lot at the time compared to other investments, but this was an investment for America. War bonds became the one thing everybody of every age had to have.

Eight times the United States government organized bond drives during World War II, generating $185 billion in revenue. That sum, equivalent to $2 trillion of 2012 money, was 60 percent of the expenditures necessary to fight the conflict. Eight times Americans turned out in droves supporting the national cause, buying through outright purchase or payroll deduction as the bonds were issued. In Medina County, it was a cause that bordered on fanaticism.

Today, we sell concessions at band concerts or Christmas trees on the north side of the square in town. In January 1942, it was home to the Million Dollar House, the bond headquarters. Within six weeks of Pearl Harbor, Medina Countians had purchased more than $100,000 of bonds. By the end of February another $100,000, and by year's end, $1 million of war bonds could be found in this county. They kept on buying everywhere a bond salesman or woman could be found.

The employees at A.I. Root and Permold might have supported Dewey, but they bought into Roosevelt's bond idea every week with payroll deductions, and Dallas Warner's wife gave her entire paycheck to the effort. The nickel going for lunch at the elementary school went to a class bond instead, and Ella Schrock mobilized her friends at the high school to do even more. Seven days a week, Amherst Spitzer, county bond chairman, made sure that the office was open and staffed to meet demand, and Charlie Griesinger tried to get every business in town to get on the payroll deduction bandwagon. After all, it was all going to pay off. The people of Medina had done so much that they were about to finally find out who really was on first.

At about 7:00 p.m. on Wednesday, August 19, 1943, with virtually every resident of Medina County jammed onto the town square, the car that had come down Route 3 from Cleveland pulled to a stop—the kings of comedy, Abbot and Costello, had arrived. It was the U.S. Treasury Department's gift to the people of Medina County, the great team performing their favorite routines for a town that had and would do so much to fund a war.

Once upon a time, from in front of a building we now drive right past, in a town that gave millions in the name of duty and was about to give even more that money couldn't buy.

Fought by Men, Won by Women

June 28, 2012

It was a war fought by men and won by women, this World War II. In a little-realized fact, there is more administration than attack in a military organization. With the outbreak of hostilities, the United States military brass quickly realized that paperwork was the enemy of the fighting man more than the Japanese or the Germans. Too much manpower in the office took manpower from the front lines. To its credit, the American military saw the solution in the nation's strongest asset: woman power.

With the first bombs at Pearl Harbor, Americans remembered that war is total, not limited action engagement. Total war is horrific, a slaughter of humanity being the true objective. Into that inferno would be cast the medical profession, better suited to administering shots than stitching bullet wounds. It would be a job for saints known as nurses.

The American aid system was carefully organized, in theory, even before war broke out. There would be corpsmen to treat the wounded on the front line and an evacuation system back to a battalion aid station. From there, it

Just another of the women of the war off to victory. *Sharon Beachy Collection.*

was to a regimental field hospital, supposedly as close as nurses would come to combat. Serious cases continued the evacuation, the worst cases being shipped back to hospitals in the United States or its territories. It gave some young ladies from Medina a firsthand look at real war as the angels known as nurses.

Helen Smathers found the war in a place called Bataan, but for Blanche Sigman, it was at a landing near Anzio. These were not the sanitary conditions of Crile Hospital but the mud and filth of true combat and the horrors that go with it. Smathers would escape to live happily ever after, but not every nurse could make that claim. In both the army and the navy, the nurses served as commissioned officers, but no rank or pay could measure up to the duty they performed. They were the gallant ones, nearly forgotten as the noble women of the WAAC and the WAVES.

The Women's Army Auxiliary Corps (WAAC) was formed in March 1942 and was replaced by the Women's Army Corps (WAC) for the duration. It was the "all other" of army duties, its ranks filled to become the secretaries, file clerks, motor pool drivers and all other bureaucratic duties to be assigned. Uniformed, subjected to their own variety of basic training and advanced education, the WAAC/WAC troopers were a military unit performing what is today civilian government service.

River Styx resident Mary Leidig was the first WAAC of Medina County, enlisting soon after the corps was formed. Unlike most WAAC troops who would remain stateside during the war, Leidig was transferred to North Africa after Basic, maintaining an overseas post office. Advancing through the ranks, she would spend twenty-two months not far from Rommel, ending her duties as a decorated tech of the motor pool before coming back home.

For Evelyn Underwood, khaki just wasn't the color, far preferring the blues of the WAVES to be Medina County's first recruit for that service. As a member of the Women Accepted for Voluntary Emergency Services in the navy, the new recruit had the same opportunities as her counterparts in the WAAC/WAC and then some. Understanding that this was not college and that the recruits were not after MRS degrees, the navy of World War II was the first to let some of the ladies play with numbers and with guns.

Numbers for the navy sought out women mathematically inclined or those with an aptitude for crossword puzzles within the WAVES for special duty. These would be the truly unknowns, the clericals of the cryptography department within Naval Intelligence, the code-breakers of both fronts. Guns for the sharp-eyed, navy officials quickly realizing that a former schoolteacher was quite capable of communicating the concepts of aim, direction and target identification on the artillery ranges. Just some of the unusual occupations women wanting to serve would find in the duty to a nation.

Once upon a time, it was a war fought by men and won by women, in stateside service and across the seas. Some of it was boring work, some of it terrifying, but it was a call answered without question or hesitation. It is unfortunate, as we do treasure those veterans still left, that we too often look past their loving spouses who were just as brave, just as heroic. The Greatest Generation, men and women alike who sometimes never saw what was right on front of them.

SUPER SECRET FROM MEDINA

August 16, 2012

The easiest way to hide the greatest secrets is to place them out in plain sight for everyone to see. It is human nature; we accept people going about their business as having some obvious purpose. That everyone is exactly where they should be and doing exactly what they should be doing. We don't want to make waves, and so we don't ask questions. That's why the good people of Medina in 1944 missed the greatest secret on earth.

After all, it was right there in the print of the April 7 edition of the *Gazette*. Just another piece of war news, another local boy going off to join the ranks of the military. There'd been hundreds of reports just like it in the newspaper ever since December 7, 1941. Somebody volunteered, somebody got drafted, somebody was commissioned an officer and somebody else was a nurse. It was all duly reported, a name, hometown in the county and where the inductee was heading next. It all made good reading even if one piece didn't quite make perfect sense.

He was a good kid, this Neil Kenneth Dickinson of Medina High School class of 1925. Smart—an outstanding student in fact—besides being a good-looking guy. Most of the community knew him for all the right reasons. A fine young man of great potential to do anything he cared to do was the local opinion. On that April 7, 1944, nobody was surprised that the good guy was off to be an officer in the United States Navy. Lieutenant Junior Grade Neil K. Dickinson was reporting for service with the navy in Knoxville, Tennessee.

We who were never good in geography in school might not have thought much about the simple statement. Those of us who actually have been to Knoxville might have been curious for a moment, recalling rivers, streams, creeks and an occasional lake but no naval base necessity. In Medina of 1944, nobody thought anything at all about the unusual posting. After all, it was a world war, it was the government and it was the navy.

For the first time in the lives of the people of Medina County, places across the world became real, not just dots on a map. It truly was a universal conflict, men and women from the area encircling the globe. Places schoolchildren once only knew as an answer to a spelling bee were now a battleground. The earth had become a very small place suddenly, and until the Axis Powers were defeated, it would shrink by the day.

Pork-barrel politics was not created by the venerable West Virginia Senator Robert Byrd, although he could well have perfected the art. Even during World War II, the nature of the political beast continued to pass out rewards for support or pet projects that could border on the irrational. To the citizens of Medina reading the newspaper, a naval base on top of the hills of eastern Tennessee wasn't any more unusual than a Coast Guard base in eastern West Virginia today. With politics, nearly all things are possible, but there was consolation. After all, it was the navy.

Britannia might have thought it ruled the waves, but after June 1942, at a place called Midway, the American Navy truly did. Three-dimensional warfare of air, surface and submariner tactics was perfected by the noble descendants of John Paul Jones then as it is now by the mightiest fighting force on earth. From its strength had come the confidence of the people it protected—that if the navy dictated, it must be right, even when it chose to set sail in Knoxville, Tennessee.

The good people of Medina didn't give Neil Dickinson much more thought in 1944 or even as the war came to a conclusion in Europe. A lot of the locals were coming home, a few never would and an odd posting in the *Gazette* had been forgotten, at least until the week before the Japanese surrender and Lieutenant Dickinson could be mentioned one last time. His work was finally done. Little Boy had made sure of that.

Lieutenant Dickinson hadn't actually been stationed at Knoxville but rather nearby at a place called Oak Ridge, Tennessee, employed in the greatest secret in the history of World War II: the atomic bomb. The chief research engineer of reflect technology on the world's most frightening weapon, and nobody knew a thing. Perhaps that was because a whole community was out and about collecting junk.

In the Cause of Scrap

August 23, 2012

It was America's first recycling drive, and the entire nation was about to go green. Olive drab green. For one brief moment, the United States turned its attention to an environmental situation and set to work eliminating a particular kind of pollution—the pollution of the enemy. It all began with what everyone had already thrown away. Within days of the attack at Pearl Harbor, the Great Medina Scrap Iron Drive was underway.

Production methods were quite different in the years leading up to World War II from what they are today. In 2012, we rely on plastics, compositions, synthetics and aluminum for most of our daily essentials. In 1941, car bodies were made of metal, radios of wood and eyeglasses actually had glass. With the declarations of war, metal was going to have a higher priority than making a kitchen stove. It was all going off to battle.

By government decree, metal for civilian production was reduced by 50 percent with the outbreak of hostilities. Resources that would have created a 1943 Pontiac were shipped to a naval yard on the coast instead. It was a policy met with universal acceptance, with the entire nation united as never before or since. The American people well understood that it would be a matter of make-do for the duration, and even that might not be enough. It was time for the American farmers to step up and lead the way.

Under the direction of the Agricultural Defense Board, local plow-pushers were to collect any and all unused and/or broken farm equipment for the scrap pile. Any piece of any size was fair game for the collection, as nothing was too small for our boys in the service. As one of the nation's largest consumers of metal, the agriculturalists were predicted to be able to provide hundreds of pounds of metal for the war effort. It quickly became obvious that it wasn't hundreds of pounds—it was tons.

In Medina County alone, the 3,124 farmers on record in 1941 assembled fifty-eight tons of scrap in the first two months of the war plus an apology to local board chairman Everett Adams. If there hadn't been some of the worst snowstorms on record in January, there would have been even more collected for the cause. It was a noble effort duly reported in the *Gazette* and caught the imagination and the efforts of the entire community.

At High's Jewelers, the movement brought in more than two hundred watch cases, all donated to the melt-down process. At Weymouth School, the average collection in the first three months of the war was two hundred pounds per student. At Medina High School, the senior class assembled forty-five tons in the name of victory. Hundreds of pounds turned into hundreds of tons in the first six months of war, and it just kept coming.

Using the local grain mills as assembly points, metal from nearly every household came together. It was a model of transportation efficiency: a piece of scrap in a yard was picked up, put in a truck, taken to a grain mill and put on a train to be assembled with scrap from other communities. From there, it was either east or west, by Lake Erie or other trains, all within a matter of days. Within weeks, all was melted down and a new life had begun.

What had been plows and iron wheels became the metal that would make howitzers and helmets in the smelting pots of the mills. The blast furnaces across the country thawed the last iceberg of the Great Depression, proving once again that war is good business. America was back to work seven days a week, at a fever pitch to defeat Tojo and Hitler in one fell swoop. There were no sacrifices that the local citizens could make that were too great in late 1941, especially when it came to that old junk in the cellar.

Spring Grove Cemetery had given up its decorative cannon, and the locals followed suit and turned Grandpa's firearms to the cause of scrap—the old rifles and pistols that had fought in the Revolution, in the Civil War, at San Juan Hill and at the Marne. In today's market, more than $5 million in war relics became the essentials of war again, without regret, for the cause. A cause to return a world to where it needed to be.

The homefront of 1941 understood that the cost of freedom has nothing to do with dollars. It is always all about duty and, once in a while, a little bit of diligence, especially when it came to the neighbors.

THE JAPANESE INVASION OF MEDINA

August 30, 2012

It's called political correctness, taking the events of another time and attempting to force current viewpoints on a bygone era. At best it is mindless; at worst it creates revisionist history, but it has, does and will go on as long as somebody somewhere has an agenda to push. Should that be in doubt, just ask Tom Hanks.

That Tom Hanks, the talented thespian who gives full credit to the Cleveland Shakespearian Festival for launching his career and who is quite capable of Forrest Gump logic as well. In the process of promoting his project, a *Band of Brothers* set in the Pacific Theater, Hanks made the incredibly foolish statement that the American involvement against the Japanese was a reflection that this was a purely racial war begun by Americans. Unfortunately for the actor, historic facts seem to say something else.

A small fact like the issue that the Japanese attacked the United States at Pearl Harbor and the Philippines on December 7, 1941, tends to be glossed over in a correct world. So, too, is the fact the Japanese had already been at war four years before that Sunday morning, locked in a death struggle with their mortal enemies, the Chinese. It is difficult to claim Anglo-Saxon arrogance over an inferior peoples as a root cause given those two events. At least we as a nation did give the politically correct–oriented the opportunity to belittle the nation. We had Executive Order 9066.

By any set of 2012 standards, this edict of the Roosevelt administration was the most egregious violation of Constitutional liberties in the history of America. Thousands of citizens were rounded up and would spend most of the war interred in prison camps for the simple offense of being of Japanese heritage. Although there were a few German and Italian citizens also incarcerated, the burden of guilt without crime fell to Asian citizens. It is a hideous miscarriage as long as we don't care to discuss September 12, 2001.

Short memories are not an American phenomenon, but we have perfected the art. We can't seem to recall now that the day after the World Trade murders, almost every citizen of the United States with Middle Eastern heritage was immediately branded a Taliban. They were all enemies to the state, and so it was in the aftermath of Pearl Harbor. The government overreacted in 1941, of that there is no doubt, but it was an overreaction for the safety of those citizens whose rights were denied—even those citizens who got away.

It is a little-known footnote to World War II that not every Japanese American on the West Coast spent the war in a prison camp. In fact, several hundred sailed away from San Francisco on the ship *Gripsholm*, willingly bound for a return to life under the emperor in Japan. Many more would serve in the European Theater with the 442nd Combat Group, fighting in Italy. The Japanese Americans were overwhelmingly American Japanese, but we are a cautious people. Especially when the Nagahashi family came to Medina.

The good citizens knew they were coming, as the *Gazette* had made it perfectly clear. On a small farm outside Brunswick, they worked during the war, all the time under the watchful eye of careful neighbors. There were laws in effect—enemy aliens had to register and give up their radios and any firearms. The sheriff was watching, too; up to now, the only aliens in the area weren't anybody's enemy. These strangers were "the Japs," though, at least according to the paper. Finally, after several months, one of the neighbors struck up a conversation with the Nagahashi family. What he discovered was a terror worse than anyone could have ever feared.

There is no accounting for the views and opinions of other people some time. Despite all logical argument or common sense, there will always be some who hold to a view that defies all sanity, that offends all morals of a community. When the curious neighbor reported the facts he learned, Medina County to a man was outraged. Not because the Nagahashi family supported the emperor; they didn't. They couldn't even speak Japanese, not even "Good morning" in that foreign tongue. Their crime was even greater: they were born and raised in Michigan and still thought Wolverine football was the best in the Big Ten.

Some things will never change, whether the war is in the Pacific or at the Horseshoe, for us Buckeyes who never shall bleed Maize and Blue.

THE LEGEND OF THE COUNTY HOME

September 6, 2012

He was the master of the dance floor—the two-step, the foxtrot and the waltz—an art form for the expert. Moving around the hardwood was as natural as his ability to play the drums in the house dance band. Any visitor to the Medina County Home in the past twenty-five years knew the great Finn Dietrich, but very few knew the actual truth. Right there at the county's oldest health institution lived one of the great heroes of World War II.

Not that such a thing was ever his intention; it just all worked out that way for a young man who hadn't even heard of Medina County once upon a time. In fact, he'd barely heard of a place called the United States outside of geography class. It was just a distant land, far away from Finn's home in Norway. Life should have been so simple for the skinny lad who so loved woodworking. Simplicity ended on April 9, 1940, for Finn and all of Norway. The Germans arrived.

They called it Operation Weserübung, the Third Reich's invasion of both Norway and Denmark. Using a planned British and French invasion of Norway as a pretext, the Germans struck first, moving quickly against little organized military resistance and forcing the capitulation of both nations in a matter of days. Preventing an enemy attack was the least of the benefits to Hitler's minions. Securing Norway, the Germans had access to the Atlantic through the Baltic Sea, as well as the heavy water of the Norsk Hydro plant, an essential element to atomic research. With the war in the palm of their hand, the Germans had also unleashed their greatest enemy: the Underground.

Like the Belgians, the Dutch and the Yugoslavs, the Norwegian Resistance was truly everything the French claimed to be. It was more than cat-and-mouse games with the occupying Germans. A cat will usually play a little with its prey before the inevitable. For the Resistance, it was a matter of kill or be killed each and every time a bridge was blown up, a truck ambushed or a phone line cut. It was a world of sleeping with both eyes open, especially when the Germans figured out that Finn Dietrich was definitely not just an ordinary Joe.

At least the followers of Hitler gave the future Medina resident a marvelous sendoff, an absolute surprise party that included the Germans breaking down the front door of a Resistance safe house as Finn ran out the back. There was the obligatory chase through the woods and then time for water sports, with Finn swimming for his life as the German farewell cards came in the form of bullets splashing around him. Such is the life of a young man whose hobbies included attacking German convoys. God does shine on the just, as a freighter nearby rescued the young lad and quickly set sail for a whole new world, a much better place than Norway in 1940.

In was in Canada where Finn made his next home, at least for a few months, as he pursued a new occupation. Instead of turning wood, he was turning propellers as a pilot in training. In July 1941, nearly a year after his escape from Norway, Finn visited Great Britain on an extended stay, part of the axe head of the Royal Air Force 332nd Squadron. It was time to take the war back to the Germans.

Out of a base in northern Scotland, behind the controls of a Spitfire, Finn and his squadron mates patrolled the airways near the Low Countries. The future County Home legend was not a participant in the Battle of Britain, the Norwegians arriving after that had ended. Finn was not an ace, never confirming the downing of five enemy aircraft. He was just an eyewitness from five thousand feet above to the greatest moment in World War II history. Finn Dietrich was one of the fighter pilots providing cover over the beaches of Normandy on D-Day.

After the war, the 332nd Squadron returned to the Norwegian air force, continuing to fly to this day in the defense of that nation. For Finn, though, there was no more military career after the German surrender. Instead, it was a life in a new world that ended just a few months ago, a life that spread incredible happiness wherever he went, even in a County Home. A man always willing to give, although not quite as much as one woman was willing to sacrifice to hit the target.

AT THE EXPENSE OF FASHION

September 13, 2012

There is nothing like a world war to totally alter the American lifestyle. To consider the changes in this nation between 1941 and 1945 is to think of shortages, rationing and the horrible cost in human lives. There was another change, though, often forgotten but never overlooked even today on streets all around the country. World War II was about to forever change that marvelous thing called women's fashion.

The stodgy remnants of Victorian primness had entered their death throes immediately after the First World War. Throughout the 1920s, hair and hemlines grew shorter, as did the old folks' patience with the younger generation. It was a time of high misdemeanors and low morals, at least according to the patriarchs of families; it was a world of promiscuity and abuses humanity couldn't get enough of. The Great Depression of the 1930s reformed society, returning modesty and virtue to the arsenals of many young ladies. Hems lowered, sanity returned and then came Pearl Harbor to give us the start of what we have today.

First to go was the treasured silk stockings that had become such a part of the properly dressed woman. It was a material better suited for parachutes opening over Africa and then Europe than shapely legs of Medina in the name of the war effort. It wasn't long before everyday wear followed suit, with hemlines shorter and material much simpler in support of the cause. Shortly after the shooting started, even hemlines didn't matter—all because of Rosie the Riveter.

It was a moment of societal adjustment in the United States, this outbreak of war. Women had only begun the steps to equality twenty years before the beginning of the conflict with the right to vote. Now some were making more steps toward that goal in the military, while many more walked on in the world of labor. With men off to fight, the former secretaries and clerks were becoming production workers, punching a clock in the factories and running machinery, not a steno notebook. It was a world where dresses and skirts very quickly became something for the weekend.

Loy, Dietrich and Hepburn had put them in the movies, but now slacks, trousers and dungarees became part of a majority of women's wardrobes across America. Today's everyday essential was shocking at first, with women becoming men in the older generation's eyes. It wasn't just that their legs disappeared; women of the time also now smoked in public, went to bars and acted like there was nothing they couldn't do. America was changing forever, even down to the hairstyles.

Gone were the days of the uncut hair carefully braided and wrapped into a bun or over the head. The finger wave of the film became the style of the workingwoman, whether in the factory or still in the office. Shoulder length was considered long by 1943, so much easier to take care of for the thoroughly modern woman. Only the old grannies clung to outdated styles like waist-length hair. Old ladies and Hazel.

Hazel Marie Smith of Wadsworth was never much for fashion. She made do when the styles started to change, but it wasn't a real high priority to wear the shortest skirts or gabardine slacks. She just liked her hair long, with almost a fleck of red in the brunette tresses when the sun was right. Still, there was a war on, and there were sacrifices to be made, even sacrifices that gave one young lady a commendation.

Hazel was still getting used to her short hair when the letter came from Freiz Instruments thanking her for the donation of her locks to the cause. It didn't make a lot of sense how hair could "aid the needs of science and industry" to serve the war requirements for some subsidiary of Bendix Aviation. It was just hair, hair that would grow back. Hazel just didn't understand how it could be important even as she didn't know she was dropping the payloads over Berlin, Schweinfurt, Aachen and throughout the South Pacific.

That long hair of Hazel Marie Smith of Wadsworth did more than most of America could ever dream during World War II. It was one of the nation's greatest military secrets until well after the shooting stopped. The beautiful brunette locks of a small-town girl were the crosshairs of the Norden bombsight in B-17s around the world. Just another contribution from one of many unlikely heroes who always claimed that they'd done nothing at all.

UNCLE SAM WANTED HIM

September 20, 2012

He could have been the most popular man in America during World War II if anybody had known who he was. For Ken Lipstreau, it was just his tiny contribution to the war effort. They made him a soldier in name only, his duty to service doing what came so naturally to him, being the artist. For the duration, he would be stationed at Fort Lee, Virginia, cleaning his brushes and not an M-1. To the day he died, he maintained that he'd done nothing really, even if history might see it differently.

Any Medina County resident who was around during the Bicentennial Celebration in 1976 knew Ken Lipstreau. He was the artist who created the commemorative series of historical prints that still grace many the home and office in the area. From his studio at his house beside the Medina County Historical Society, the master created wonders in oil based on the past and fleshed out by the people he met. It was just something to do, just like his time in the service. He'd been just a painter, but his brother, Duff…now there was a hero.

It must have taken more physical agility than allowed by law for long, tall Duff Lipstreau to wedge himself into a B-17, even as a young man. He'd done well at Basic, well enough that he was assigned to advanced training as a bombardier before the 8th Army Air Corps headed off to England. He learned his craft well, with the Norden sight as natural to him as chewing gum. Duff Lipstreau became one of those kids who really could drop his payload into a pickle barrel from fifteen thousand feet. One foggy morning in 1944, he found out that he was too good.

The mission was the ball bearing plants at Schweinfurt—just another day, just another massive assault, with one exception. The bombardier for the lead ship had taken sick in the night, and the next best man would have to fill in. Duff Lipstreau was called from his plane and reassigned to lead the raid from up front. Just another day, just another assault where the payloads dropped right on target and almost everybody made it home. Every ship save one: the B-17 that Duff had left to take command.

There were no chutes that opened, and there were no survivors, just the crews on either side reporting that the plane went straight down after it was hit. Somewhere in Holland, ten good kids had died, but one bombardier lived on. Duff Lipstreau would fly his twenty-five missions to earn a ticket home and then a few more on top of that for good measure. He never forgot what quirks of fate let a man live when others found eternity, but Duff Lipstreau made sure that anyone who listened knew that what he'd done was nothing; it was his brother Ken who'd been the hero.

So it is for that Greatest Generation, no matter the contribution. It was always someone else who did more. Some other pilot, some other dogface, some other stateside trooper who had made the difference. It was an entire generation of modesty, no matter the accomplishment. Fortunately for those who will always live in awe of the generation before, the proof was right on the table in front of me.

It was brother Duff who opened the folio case for me to see one afternoon, with brother Ken making himself busy doing something else, anything else. They were just some sketches and a few paintings, nothing more than that, at least according to the artist who'd drawn them. I suspect that Duff used it as a test, to see if this next generation could possibly understand history in front of it. It was a test I seemed to have passed quite well.

Millions of troopers headed off to war, drawn into service by the Draft, by their anger at the assault on America and by recruiting posters that reinforced that concept that there is no shame in serving the nation that gives life, liberty and the pursuit of happiness. Recruiting posters just like the ones in the folio before me that day. Posters and their reproductions I'd seen a thousand times, never dreaming that history lived next door.

Ken Lipstreau didn't draw the "Uncle Sam Wants You" poster; that's a fact. He drew just about all the other ones of the time, though. The creative genius, the soft-spoken next-door neighbor to the county museum, just another elderly statesman who did things the old way, the right way, just like another of the Greatest by the name of Loraine.

WITH PEN AND PAPER

October 18, 2012

It is almost a forgotten art today, the ability to write a letter. Not a text or an e-mail but rather an epistle that is actually written, by hand, on a piece of paper. We live in a world where soldiers literally in combat can Tweet or socially network from a battlefield. Seventy years ago, it was all so different, when a government could be efficient and eventually creative in the process of winning a war.

In fact, the written word must be given credit as one of the contributing factors that ensured Allied victory in World War II, the news from home being a lifeblood that kept morale up no matter how much a trooper had to keep his head down. Virtually every veteran of the conflict recalls the joy of hearing his or her name at mail call or the disappointment of a week without news from home. Simple sheets of paper that brought Smith Road and all its news to Anzio or Stavelot. The current events of Brunswick into the jungle of New Guinea. The mail service of World War II was a study of American strategic ingenuity.

For the first time in military history, the United States mail was no longer private, whether he be private or general. Airmail sent, censor approved. *Sharon Beachy Collection.*

In theory, it was a perfect concept—mail to and from soldiers overseas would be funneled through Army Post Offices (APOs) on the East and West Coasts. Long before zip codes, individual divisions would be assigned their own identification number. Blake Friedt's family in Medina could write their letter, put it in an envelope, address it to the private at APO 30 in New York and know that it would get there for the price of a domestic stamp. Russ Hershberger's family in Homer had the same luxury, knowing that APO 251 would find its way to the 1st Armored Division, wherever it might be. It was a marvelous theory of delivery that nearly collapsed literally under its own weight.

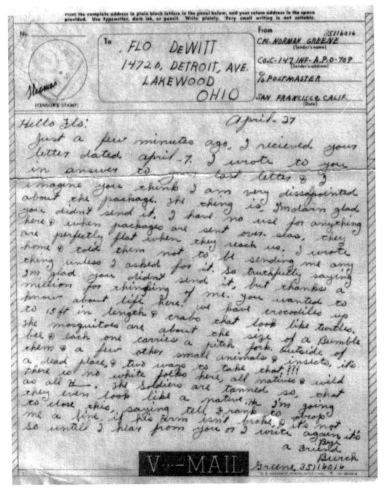

V-Mail, the microfilm answer to the tons and tons of letters home from all fronts in World War II. *Sharon Beachy Collection.*

Much to the chagrin of the theorists, the mail became much more than a matter of family convenience; it became a matter of civic duty. It was almost un-American to not have a serviceman or servicewoman as a pen pal, as well as writing to every family member who might be stationed away from home. The thousands of letters that a peacetime Army Post Office handled before December 7, 1941, suddenly became millions. Two million one-ounce letters that would have a total weight of nearly sixty-three tons of paper. The brilliant concept of military mail almost stopped, severing the only lifeline the dogface would have to home, but American know-how was about to save the day.

They called it V-Mail, the brainchild of the Eastman Kodak Company in Rochester, New York. Letters were opened, photographed, put onto microfilm sheets and then sent. Upon arrival at the destinations across the world, the film was printed and then distributed. Instead of sixty-three tons of cargo space on a ship, the same amount of correspondence weighed in at about 1,200 pounds. It was pure brilliance that made life much easier for everybody save one: the censor.

Much to the surprise and chagrin of today's human rights advocates, every single piece of mail sent by a U.S. serviceman during the height of World War II was read by somebody else besides the intended recipient. G.I.s were like our Congress—they told everything they knew, truth or not. As a matter of military security, dates and places were clipped or blackened out by G-2 staffs all around the world during the war. Although there was never a letter completely deleted, a few did come close, and more entertained for their somewhat erotic content. The military never could tell who else might want to know this or that, even until virtually the last day of the war. Seventy years later, and it's all technology now, almost.

Yet there still remain isolated pockets of the old school, where writing beautiful letters about the news of the day still exists. The Amish are masters of it, but so too is my sweetheart, who is one of the Greatest Generation. Every two weeks, this eyewitness to those times of World War II writes me, the script still perfect, the thoughts so sincere. Every two weeks I, too, get to have some feeling of what those boys at the Bulge or Tarawa must have so looked forward to with every mail call.

Thank you, my dear Loraine. This one was inspired by you, yet another priceless gem who will live forever—in my heart, in these pages and in the beautiful letters you write to this day.

A Lady with a Past

November 15, 2012

She was quietly kind, if that makes any sense. It's been thirty years since we talked, but I still remember that trait from that only time we met. It was at an art show at the Our Lady of Bethlehem Convent School on the Olentangy River Road in Columbus. I was looking at some sixth grader's interpretative creation when she came over, just making conversation and appreciating a visitor. Miss Mildred, the language teacher there in 1982—yet another of the multitude of civilians who had done so much in World War II.

Her modesty was becoming; what she had done during the war was nearly forty years' past. People weren't really interested anymore. It was much more exciting to talk about art or the piano recital that was coming up. Miss Mildred knew all the children as if they were her own; that was the issue of the day. There was a shy smile and almost a blush when a passerby assumed that she was one of the sisters of the order. Almost a joke too, as her cloistered life inside the convent was really no different than a nun's given the lack of men around. Still, on this day, it was all about the art of a brush, even though once it had all been so different. Once upon a time, Miss Mildred was an artist with words.

Forty years before, she'd been the queen of the airways for the GIs in England, the nightly broadcasts being a touch of home mingled in with news, gossip and tunes of the day. The soft-spoken teacher once could make butter melt, her tones so smooth and her laughter so sincere. There wasn't a dogface who didn't know that golden voice, tuning in every evening to catch up and daydream of that glorious day when everybody could go home.

My father used to listen, although he went to his grave maintaining that Miss Mildred played far too much of the Dorsey brothers and not enough Glenn Miller. Most of his tent mates thought that she talked too much, too much filler in the air, but Dad didn't have a problem with it. Like today, guys back then weren't always interested in the news of the day but rather were more in touch with mindless entertainment. It gave the troopers something to argue about, every soldier's duty and right. Miss Mildred just kept on doing what she always did, and the GIs kept hoping that just once she might mention them.

It was a feature, not every night but from time to time, that Miss Mildred would single out units for special recognition. Once in a great while, some Shavetail second lieutenant might hear his name as well, although usually it took a major's cluster or higher to rate the privilege. Dad and the guys in the 291st Combat Engineers never made the air, but the troops next door did after the breakout in 1944. That led to some good-natured ribbing all around, just something to fill in the monotony of a war going on all around then—a war during which Miss Mildred stayed with the boys almost all the way to the finish.

Things happened fast those last few months of the war, and nobody really had much time to do anything but keep on moving. The Brits and Yanks were crashing in from the west and the Russians from the east, and Europe was just trying to get out of the mess alive. The surrender came, troops rushed home and promises to keep in touch were long forgotten in a new world being created—a new world that rapidly left Miss Mildred far behind.

In that different world Miss Mildred found a life, never to be on the air again after the war in Europe was over. There were some issues to be resolved throughout the 1950s, her life not really finding contentment until she came to the convent. A certain inner happiness I wasn't about to disturb by doing anything but talking about elementary school art and a recital coming up. We didn't talk of the past, only the day, and I never did say anything to Dad about the meeting. After all, I knew who Mildred really was to the Allied armies of World War II.

Miss Mildred Gillars, who spent World War II on the radio broadcasting propaganda from Berlin as Midge, still today mistaken as Axis Sally, the most hated woman on earth by the boys who went to war from little old Medina County and the woman who died so quietly kind and without a single regret.

Bad Advice Not Taken

December 20, 2012

It's been 110 years ago now, with the Wright brothers still trying to find North Carolina on a map, when Medina's Ross Schlabach answered the call of his Uncle Sam. He was just a kid back in 1902, but he knew that life didn't center on little old Medina County. There was someplace else he needed to be and only one way to get there for a boy who saw the future. A bright young man who understood perfectly how the world turned. The future and the world would soon belong to the United States Navy.

The nation's oceangoing forces had burst onto the world stage as one century ended and another began. First it was around Cuba, driving overmatched Spanish forces back across the Atlantic one last time. Then it was on to the Far East, quelling the Philippines Insurrection before moving on to yet another forgotten war, the Boxer Rebellion in China. For the moment, *Britannia* still ruled the waves, but it was by prestige alone that it held the crown. American technology was at sail in the ultimate rise to the top, and Ross Schlabach wasn't going to be left out.

Over the next forty years, Schlabach would sail on virtually every classification of ship the navy could put to water and endure duty in almost every port imaginable. He survived the drudgery of weather station duty and the excitement of the American Expeditionary Force's arrival to World War I's inferno. As he rose slowly in rank, the Medina native son learned his life lessons on everything from tender to battleship before the War to End All Wars had concluded. Twenty years later, when it was Captain Schlabach, he even had some carrier experience. More importantly, though, he'd learned to be Old Navy.

A skipper who didn't know every bolt of his ship and every crewman's weakness didn't last long at sea in the navy between the wars. There were too many other bright young officers trying to scale the ladder for even the smallest cruiser's commander to become complacent. The Great War was over, never to happen again. Budget cuts and public opinion made the navy, and every other branch of service, border on the expendable. A captain's proficiency reports had to be top notch, or an old salt might well find himself selling shoes stateside in the thinking of the mid-1930s. Captain Ross Schlabach wasn't about to let that happen. After all, he'd just figured out that other part of being Old Navy that was more important than any seaborne chart. It was the art of navigating the cocktail party.

The social scene of the peacetime navy before World War II rivaled all of high society's finest moments in the most wealthiest of communities. There was no extravagance too great and no liquor too rare for the proper host and hostess seeking a few moments with the admiral, whatever admiral it might be. It was a world Captain Schlabach of Medina knew, but not as well as he knew his ship apparently. He never did make the right connections to get his own admiral's star. Instead, he had to settle for the personal friendship of Frank Knox, the secretary of the navy.

So close was the friendship that Secretary Knox sought the advice of Captain Schlabach on a matter of the gravest importance: the secretary's daughter had been seeing this pilot, that sort of thing. The captain knew the young lady, he knew the air jockey and he knew they had no future. Just another rank-seeking hotshot—that's all the kid would ever be, of that there was no doubt. The young man didn't have any sense, even for a navy pilot. After all, he'd gone to school at Michigan. No doubt at all of Captain Schlabach's wisdom.

The young lady did marry her sweetheart, who came home to her after the war and set off for a new life. They had children, with the son Thomas catching a lot of compliments about his looks when he was born in 1951. In fact, he still does, even as he's now on a career of his own. A career catching criminals on television as a character by the name of Leroy Jethro Gibbs—Thomas Mark Harmon's secret little tribute to his grandfather, the secretary of the navy during World War II, on today's CBS hit show *NCIS*.

Captain Schlabach, the great captain and the good cocktail host but the most lousy relationship counselor who ever sailed the seven seas.

A FINANCIAL SOLUTION IN THE PAST

January 3, 2013

A New Year has arrived and, with it, an age-old problem. Now that the parties have ended, every American's priority this year turns to paying for last year. Unlike the Beltway's Delusionals, our obligations are real and require immediate solution. Fortunately for the thinking public, like it is with every problem, the solution really is somewhere in the past we call history. All we'll have to do to cure our debt issue is live like it's 1943 all over again.

It was the midpoint of the war for the United States, although at first it appeared to be a war that would never end. The Japanese had lost at Midway but still ran wild in the Far East. Rommel was back-pedaling after the American landing in North Africa, but Europe was still German. Millions had already died, and millions more were about to in the insanity of the time. Here in Medina County, the land of plenty had become a land without.

Living as if it were seventy years ago starts with eliminating most people's ambition this year: the new car. Beginning in January 1942, automobile production America ceased to exist for the duration of the war. The factories that had made Buicks and Chevys now turned out jeeps, tanks and half-tracks. The plants that made parts for autos now machined parts for

For five dollars, everyone could be a part of what was considered a noble effort. *Sharon Beachy Collection.*

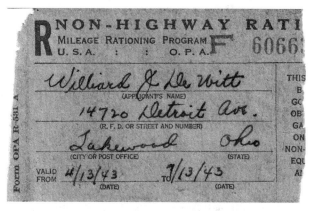

A rarity of collectibles, the R gasoline ration card. Reserved for agricultural fuel needs, they occasionally did find their way into highway use in Cleveland, Ohio. Not that any of our relations would bend the rules in time of war too much. *Sharon Beachy Collection.*

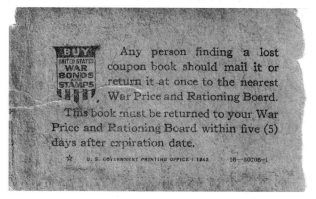

Ration books would make a great advertising tool for those most essential war bonds. *Sharon Beachy Collection.*

weapons. It was the land of full employment, but it was a nation where travelers were going to have to make do with the cars they had. By the start of 1943, making that used car last was going to be more of an issue than we can imagine today.

Fortunately, the war-era drivers of Medina County didn't have to contend with the tire-flattening debris field of today's Lake Road near the recycling center. By government regulation, one of the very first items commandeered for military use were rubber tires. On February 1, 1942, production of new passenger car tires was ended, and motorists expected to get by on used or recapped rubber for the duration. Considering what came next on the nationally mandated rationing program, it might as well have been steel wheels. Nobody was going to be driving anywhere anyway. Not on four gallons of gasoline a week.

Not for one trip. Not for one morning. Four gallons of gas was the federally mandated limit for registered cars and their owners for an entire week as 1943 began. All petroleum was desperately needed for the military, a need that would continue virtually to the end of the war on both fronts. It was considerably cheaper to live in Medina during the war than it is now, and cost cutting had only begun.

As incredible as it may seem to the modern world, eating out twice a day was not a proposition for the citizenry of Medina County in 1943. Fast food was defined as dinner eaten in less than an hour. Route 42 was not the home to every chain restaurant in America. In fact, during World War II, to eat out more than seven times a week was to surrender your food ration book to the restaurant owner for his use. There would be no sugar, coffee, liquor or a number of other staples for the home for that pleasure of dining out on checkered tablecloths. It was a choice for the consumer that didn't favor the short-order cook. Back in 1943, Americans across the country and right here as well had decided that it was far better to stay home.

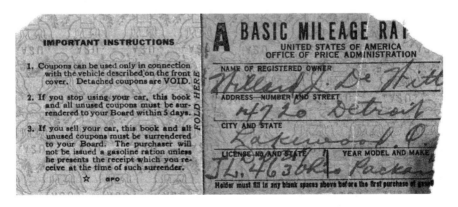

The A ration coupon—all this to get four gallons of gas per week. *Sharon Beachy Collection.*

Home without television, Internet, stereo, cellphones, videogames, CB radio or even the electric can opener, all of which had yet to be invented. It was night after night listening to a radio, reading a newspaper or actually talking to one another, as well as the neighbors, that passed the time. A simple life that, if led today, would solve every debt. It was absolutely a time of basic necessities in every single life with one purpose and, in the end, one result.

For one brief moment, it was not about me, me, me; it was about *us*. This nation rose up and acted as one, the sole purpose being a victory over evil that we even today cannot fully comprehend, even though we knew it was wrong. The result, the undeniable proof that they were the Greatest, even if they might never know what it meant to sip a latte. How lucky they were, how incredibly ignorant we can be, even in these highest of tech and best of living times today.

A Thread to the Past

January 24, 2013

Across London today, there's a movement afoot as a younger generation prepares for a weekend back in time. They are already combing the thrift stores and vintage clothiers throughout that sprawling metropolis looking for that one totally authentic, totally real piece that will make them the hit of the show. The greatest show all of England can put on at the end of each summer, that one weekend known as the Goodwood Revival.

It is the great advantage to being a member of British peerage, to be like Lord March and own a country estate that just happens to be twelve thousand acres with a past. For the family, since the time of William the Conqueror, the rural retreat was a Royal Air Force base during World War II. In 1948, Lord March's grandfather suddenly took an interest in motor as well as horse racing—enough of an interest that he built his own racetrack for cars around the perimeter of the grounds and grass circuit for horses near the mansion. Within a year, both were sites for international events, a tradition that lasted until the 1960s, when cars became too fast and horses too expensive. Twenty years later, his grandson Charles realized that there is great fun to living in the past.

On the last weekend of August, they come to Goodwood, out to capture something of a past they either lived or have dreamed about. Last year, 250,000 spectators came through the gates in three days. Travelers from all across Great Britain, the Continent, the former Soviet Union, the United States and even the seven nations of Africa were represented among the throng. Their reward was one of the greatest shows on earth and in the skies.

There were sports car races with classifications for everything from a 1909 Damiler and its contemporaries to the Cobras that ran at LeMans in the mid-1960s. It was not the parade driving so common in the American Vintage Sports Car Club of America events—this was bumper-to-bumper, fender bending, push-your-opponent-out-of-the-way, full-speed motor sports, where one race field boasted $50 million of value in the starting field, all the while more action swirled around and over the grounds.

Being a former RAF base, it was only right that Lord March arranged what he modestly called a "little air demonstration" for his guests. Ten original Spitfires that once flew in the Battle of Britain escorted a Blenheim bomber that put payloads over the sub pens of France into the airport and then showed that they were still the queens of the sky all weekend long. There were also hill climb events, speed trials, horse racing on the original grounds, music, food and a fine time to be had by all. Most of all, there were the people.

Of the quarter million who came to the event, fully half chose to live as much in the past as Lord March. Today's styles were out of place; it was all about the image, capturing the look of the 1960s, the '50s and, for most, living the look of the 1940s. Getting the look right made it so much easier to capture the illusion. Safely removed from the carnage of World War II, the reenactor acts to a higher moral standard, at least for the weekend, all the while looking good in those clothes that were such a find. The right thing, the truly authentic clothing that really was worn by the people of Great Britain in World War II, was found in those vintage stores and thrifts. Too bad the best in authentic isn't English.

There was a war, and there were shortages. There was the Blitz, and clothing was at a premium. Fortunately for wartime London, there was one American Red Cross chapter that understood the matter and stepped up to help. To organize what was called the Needle and Thread Society, a group of housewives joined together and sewed up clothing, shipping it off to the needy of England's capital. Hundreds and hundreds of outfits for women and children were given out of the spirit of international friendship. One of those dresses, still with the label of the society and the hand-stitched date of

1943, won Best in Costume just a few years ago at Goodwood. Authentic, but as Yank as it gets.

The Needle and Thread Society, a wartime institution of a place called Medina County, Ohio, USA.

A Dangerous Eleven-Year-Old

February 7, 2013

The world is confusing enough to the average eleven-year-old, even without adults making it all worse. Toss in the fact that it was 1942 and a world was at war, and one young man of that age in Wadsworth could well have been wondering about the sanity of humanity when the news reached him. Much to his absolute surprise, he, the God-fearing, baseball-playing ordinary kid of town had been deemed an "Enemy Alien."

Such was the disadvantageous situation in which thousands upon thousands of American citizens found themselves during the first few months of World War II, all guilty of the nearly capital offense of being first-generation Americans. The American Japanese of the West Coast would become the most notable victims of government hysteria, but Uncle Sam's irrational behavior was not limited to the Far East. In early 1942, it was the government's duty to watch out for any former Fatherland residents and their descendants almost as much as those desperados, the Italians of Wadsworth, Ohio.

Former natives of Europe's most colorful and perhaps most artistic nation had been part of the Wadsworth landscape since early in the twentieth century. They had come as the men and women who literally and figuratively built industry and commerce with their hands and with their hearts in this emerging nation. It was a tight-knit community that based values on family and religion melded into the Wadsworth fabric. It was a society meant to grow even more, as the 1920s and 1930s proved that Italy was not a country that anyone recognized anymore.

Much to the surprise of many casual scholars of the conflict from seventy years ago, many things associated with Nazi Germany were actually founded in Italy a decade before they appeared in the Fatherland. Hitler came to power in 1933, eleven years after Mussolini took control in Rome. The German SA and then SS bodyguards were ideas that came from the Italian

Black Shirts. Even what we consider to be the Hitler salute was, in fact, a Mussolini greeting first. Italy might not have had the programs that led to the Holocaust in their policies, but there were enough other similarities to evil that many ordinary citizens fled to the United States and its relative sanity—sane until there was some chance of war.

They called it the Alien Registration Act of 1940, not the first nor the last attempt of the United States government to monitor the true purpose of immigration into the country. The first such measure had been in 1798, the current political debates in the Congress being nothing more than another continuation of the same issue. Back in 1940, knowing full well that there was war coming, the government took proactive steps to fight the "fifth column," the enemy agents sure to infiltrate American life to prepare the way for invading hoards. Once the conflict had begun, it was simply a matter of enforcing what could be some of the most stupid legislation ever created.

These potential enemies of the state were ordered to report to local post offices, even in Wadsworth, Ohio. Natives of Germany as well as Italy were required to register and then surrender their weapons of war. Hundreds of radios were confiscated, as surely a foreign spy would know how to turn AM into shortwave. Firearms became government property, as did that most dangerous item, the flashlight. Flashlights were sure to be used as signal beacons for the planes soon to be flying overhead from the motherland. Of it all, it was that moment of registration that made a lifetime's impression on one eleven-year-old boy.

He watched as the postal inspector, impressed by his own position, looked down at the young man's father and then at the paperwork. A comment was made—two sons seemed to be missing. The eleven-year-old's father, a native of Italy with just a third-grade education, proudly announced that they weren't available, as they were in the service of their country, two more loyal American boys in the military. Instead of remembering the pompous government official, one eleven-year-old never forgot that thing about service.

When hard work and good fortune made him a college dean, he remembered service. For four good years, he served the city of Wadsworth. Once the eleven-year-old enemy alien, His Honor former Wadsworth Mayor Caesar Carrino, just another one of the Greatest even before he got to be a teenager.

PRODUCING VICTORY ONE SPADE AT A TIME

April 4, 2013

It is a hobby of today that was created out of the necessity of seventy years ago. The seed catalogues have arrived in the mail now, and true springtime is soon to be with us. It won't be long before patches of the backyard or community grounds will be staked out, and another gardening season will be underway with great expectations. Seventy years ago today, there was a little more urgency to the home growing projects in the county. It was all a matter of trying to survive with the help of a Victory Garden.

The first year of rationing certain foods had come and gone across America, with the citizens adjusting to a greater calling by doing without. The war was starting to turn, albeit slowly, in an Allied direction. There had been a victory on the seas at Midway and an invasion on land into North Africa. The final surrender of the enemy was in the distance, but patriotic fervor remained high. It was all about winning this war and getting on with a better world—a time when sacrifice was all so real in so many ways. For the good of the military and its needs, once again the American household reverted back to pioneer thinking. In Medina County, it was time for every home to start living off the land.

Under the overall direction of the brilliant agricultural educator O.C. Duke, housewives who were five generations removed from a life on the farm began to assemble in classrooms and meeting halls to again learn what once had come so naturally to their ancestors. Food comes from seeds, but seeds cannot grow themselves with any degree of productivity. It takes work, blister-creating, muscle-aching work to actually grow food for a family. After about the first class, O.C. Duke was beginning to realize that he might have the most difficult job of all. We Americans can be terribly forgetful.

In fact, it would take several classes and even more hands-on demonstrations for all the ladies of Medina to finally understand that seeds do not grow on a kitchen counter. They do have to be placed in the earth, but only after the earth had been prepared. It was just like a farm, only on a smaller scale. The earth had to be turned over in the early year and allowed to breathe. Clods had to be broken up and then the ground leveled off. The farmer had his plow, disk and harrow and the housewife her spade, hoe and rake. Within a few weeks, there would be plants. What came next was going to take more lectures and all the patience O.C. Duke had left.

Difficulty in telling the difference between a tomato plant and the year's crabgrass harvest is not something my B.W. invented in our first garden; it was an issue in 1943 as well. In all likelihood, thousands of pounds of produce were slaughtered under the blade of an overly enthusiastic hoe that spring and summer. Slowly but surely, the modern woman of World War II learned, and by fall, the benefit was obvious. Instead of going to the store and buying, she had produced. It was her vegetables for her family, freeing up the mega-farm products to go overseas. It truly was a victory for the Victory Garden and a boom to the economy in one way that nobody ever saw coming.

It was the last lecture of the Victory Garden series: the art and practice of canning—to take garden-fresh vegetables, cooking properly according to modern methods of the time and creating vacuum-sealed jars of the same for the long winters ahead so that households wouldn't have to buy goods better used at the battlefront. The process seemed so simple and so patriotic that it was logical that every household with a garden gave it a try. They gave it a try and managed to stimulate the economy better than any government agency or bailout ever could.

By August 1943, the sales of pressure cookers, the stovetop kitchen utensil most necessary for proper canning, had increased tenfold nationwide and twentyfold in Medina County. By the end of that same year, business in the home repair industry in the county had quadrupled, with 90 percent of their new business repairing holes in kitchen ceilings.

We never needed the Germans to drop bombs on the area; we had the housewives blowing holes enough right here in patriotic, gardening, pressure cooker–exploding Medina County, USA.

A WOMAN WITH ONE GREAT REGRET

April 18, 2013

She was America's greatest patriot in World War II, this Mrs. Meyers of Brunswick. There was no sacrifice too great that she wouldn't offer up in the name of success for the Allied cause. She planted a Victory Garden so more vegetables could go to the troops. She bought war bonds and defense stamps, she accepted rationing without complaint and she kept her spirits high, knowing it would all turn out all right. Mrs. Meyers also couldn't help but holding to one single regret as well.

It wasn't because she wasn't native American; her upbringing so many years before might have been the best thing to make her all the more loyal a citizen to the United States in the end. A half century before the outbreak of World War II, she had been a girl in Austria, the product of a dear mother and father. She had grown up in another kind of world, Europe of the turn of the twentieth century. A time of dukes and princes, where monarchies were the only form of government, where Poland and Czechoslovakia didn't exist yet and when the entire world was about to go crazy.

She was working in the kitchen that day when word came that their archduke had been assassinated during a goodwill trip to Serbia. Everyone knew that there could be no more peace, with too many of those monarchs far too ambitious for their intellects. In just a matter of what seemed like hours, the young men were gone, called up to serve their nation in the name of some cause. In the end, it was called the Great War, but to people like Mrs. Meyers, it was just the Great Slaughter.

Men and women by the hundreds of thousands were no more, killed by bullets, bombs and that hideous thing called poison gas. There was a hell, and it was Europe of 1914–18. Mrs. Meyers never regretted that the fortunes of war had turned against her homeland, even with the loss of so many neighbors, family and friends. A horrible war that had destroyed so many lives was about to give her a new one in the place called America.

With more than a little gladness, the young Austrian woman left that old world behind and joined the procession of hundreds of thousands of refugees to the United States. She would never regret that decision, even if there were quotas that limited immigration, even if there were tests to be passed and laws to be obeyed to become a member of a new world. She would be that good American. She would play by any rule they cared to make, just for the opportunity to have opportunity, even as the world began to go crazy all over again.

Mrs. Meyers was living in Brunswick when it began. She understood and would have been happy to sound the first warnings if anyone would have been intelligent enough to ask. As she read the papers, she carefully followed the reports of the chaos of Europe after the First World War. She watched with trepidation as fascist and communist forces battled in streets and in legislatures for control of the masses. More than her neighbors, she understood how the press back in her native land was twisting the truth to fit its own agenda. She knew exactly where it would all end up.

There was no regret that she couldn't stop the assaults of lies or the defenses of appeasement that became international politics of the 1930s.

Mrs. Meyers was an intelligent woman, and she knew that the forces in play were too immense, too well coordinated, too manipulative of the useful idiots who were their subjects for one woman to combat. All she could do was to wait, knowing that in the end, despite all the darkness, justice would come to the right, the noble and the just.

So she waited as the war began in 1939, with her former home now a source for evil. When the bombs fell on Pearl Harbor, she joined the cause along with every other housewife and did what she could, all the time still holding on to that one regret—a regret that didn't go away until April 30, 1945.

So sorry she was that it had been her brother and not her who gave that kid a black eye back in Austria when they were young. The kid, Adolf Hitler, once the next-door neighbor to Mrs. Meyers, so many years later the American patriot of Medina County, Ohio.

The Lost Tribe of Medina

May 2, 2013

It was a thriving community once upon a time, when the world last went to war. Today, it has vanished almost without a trace, just a few familiar names left in the phone book. An entire culture and its heritage gone, most never knowing it once existed, no one recalling where it called home. It was Medina's most interesting minority group: the Hungarians.

The fellow countrymen of Peter Lorre and Zoltan Kaparthy were late arrivals to the American fabric, but so too were many other Eastern Europeans. Too often forgotten is the fact that until November 1918, many of the countries where we proudly claim our roots did not exist. There was no Poland, Romania, Yugoslavia or Hungary as we know it until the last days of World War I. Wallachia, Moldavia, Bohemia and Bessarabia were the nations of Eastern Europe but are now long forgotten. It was the triumph of the Great War, these identities that were created, that would be our Hungarians' greatest curse.

Considering all the factions and factors surrounding the creation of new nations in the final days of and immediately after World War I, it remains a miracle that World War II did not begin about January 1, 1919. Every possible faction of the political spectrum vied for control of every nation in Europe. These were not conflicts on a legislative floor but rather armed street battles; surrendering was not an option for the participants. For all the love of nationalism, the members of our local Hungarian community were far too wise to remain in that hell that was their birthplace, especially when there was a paradise called Medina, Ohio.

To the thriving village they came, not one by one but in family groups. Very quickly they formed their own community within the Medina city limits. There was a Hungarian church and a Hungarian school, one for the faith and one for learning, and both firmly held on to the traditions and values of a faraway land. They started out as strangers in a strange land who very quickly became some of the area's most welcomed residents.

For all its melting pot reputation, America has not always been a receptive host to large numbers of immigrants, both foreign and domestic. New arrivals have been considered threats to the workplace ever since 1798, willing to take menial jobs even then to put food on the table. The already entrenched, unwilling to accept such positions, have reacted with legislation and secret societies designed to maintain the status quo. It was true with the Irish, the newly freed black, the Italian and virtually every ethnic group that came through the Golden Door, but not Medina's Hungarians. Despite having their own church and their own school, they set out immediately to be good Americans.

The Hungarian school taught their native language but put a higher priority on learning English. Hungarian families might have the perfect goulash recipe, but it was hot dogs and hamburgers every Fourth of July and turkey for Thanksgiving. When it came to work ethic, these ethnics didn't seem to understand the essential requirement of breaks, long lunches or days off. They were here to work for the boss, do a good job, pay their taxes and wave the flag of their new home. Come December 7, 1941, they were ready to do a lot more as well.

Every young man of draft age within the local Hungarian community served the nation during World War II. More importantly, the community itself turned out month after month for blood drives, bond drives and any other government-sponsored support of the war effort. When that wasn't enough, the Hungarians organized their own money raisers, contributing thousands of dollars to support the land of freedom, grateful for the opportunity to succeed—loyal Americans who made the totally right choice to get out of the old country while the getting was bad.

There was no doubt that it was horrible in those years after World War I. It got worse after 1941 for anybody back home when Hungary, formed to give freedom and justice to all, turned Nazi for the duration of the war. All the while, some of their native sons were America's Greatest, and now we don't even know where that Medina Hungarian church used to be.

Another great mystery of the thing called World War II, almost as mystifying as the concept of flying without an engine.

AN AMAZING IDEA BORN IN AN EMPTY FIELD

May 30, 2013

It is another example of American insanity, another repeating of an action again and again expecting a different outcome. We see it every day on any golf course in the area. Too much right hand and the banana ball goes out into Marlboro country. A triple bogey looks suddenly good, and we put the same swing on the same miserable ball the next time too. It's lunacy, but back in World War II, there was something else that could compete in the way of craziness, and the United States Army called it the "Hadrian."

Officially designated the CG-4A, the Hadrian was a wood and canvas albatross known as a glider. It was an airplane designed to fly just once in anger, traveling without an engine, left to air current and pilot skill to land at an objective. It is flight based on the basic assumptions that the glider could get off the ground and then get anywhere near its target. In World War II, those points were very much in doubt from beginning to end.

Loaded with troopers and/or cargo, a Hadrian was connected to a C-47 cargo plane by steel cable in order to take off. Assuming that the cable didn't break and the catches on both planes held in place, the glider would be towed to speed down a runway to launch into flight. At that point, a glider pilot's job was a matter of great skill to match the C-47 pilot's flaps and ailerons as both planes climbed to cruising speed and height. Once there, headed to battle, it all became a matter of luck.

A C-47 was never known to be the speed merchant of planes, slowed even more towing a load. Instead of one target, the cargo plane and glider now gave enemy antiaircraft fire two targets. A hit on either one was a death knell to a glider and all aboard. With more luck than can be found in the Horseshoe Casino, a glider would near a target and then be released from its cable for landing, generally in a farmer's field and at night, devoid of all lights. It was an idea that defied logic—bordering on lunacy—and it worked.

It worked in the early morning hours of June 6 across Normandy and then again a few months later at what was known as Operation Market Garden in Holland. More than thirteen thousand gliders would be produced during World War II, most sacrificed in the fields of Europe but achieving their objectives all the same, delivering men and supplies right to the battlefront. In the end, for all the doubts and the doubters, Buck Weaver had been right after all.

Back in 1919, just after the Great War, the concept of free flight was an ideal to Weaver. He'd seen the Wright brothers' first glider and knew that he could do better. He played with the idea in an open field that somebody called an airport, but he was a businessman as much as a pilot. As much as he wanted to lift off and enjoy absolute silence, Buck Weaver understood that the world wanted engines in its planes, and it wanted speed. Only a dreamer wanted to fly to enjoy. With more than a little regret, the glider plans were shelved, and Weaver moved into the future, far away from that open field.

Eventually, the idealist pilot and dreamer would end up in a place called Troy, Ohio, building planes better than anybody else at the time. By 1936, the Weaver Aircraft Company was the leading provider of commercial planes in the United States. Long before Boeing found Seattle, WACO had put Troy on the map as the aviation capital of the nation. Even then, Buck Weaver kept dreaming and experimenting on his 1919 design. By December 7, 1941, he had it perfected, and he called it the Hadrian.

For all their success, cargo gliders died with the Japanese surrender in 1945. Today, there are a few recreational gliders in the area, but nothing like WACO once produced. For that matter, WACO itself is fairly well forgotten except for those truly knowledgeable about flight. Almost as forgotten as that field where it all began right after the Great War.

That open field where a barnstormer named Weaver came up with the idea of the Hadrian glider, right off State Route 18, just west of a place called Mallet Creek in little old Medina County, USA.

An Ordinary Day at the Warehouse

July 18, 2013

July 17, 1944, was just another Monday to Alonzo Macky Martin. For the moment, he was just another guy doing his job to win the war. He wore a uniform and saluted officers, but he didn't feel like much of a sailor while he did that job. Life in the U.S. Navy was definitely not what he'd expected it to be when he signed up.

A few months before, he'd shown up at Basic, ready to save the world one engagement at a time. Macky Martin saw himself as a helmsman kind of guy, steering into battle at the admiral's orders. If not that, then working a gun on a battleship would have been fine to do his part. The life and times of wartime America said that there was something more important on Martin's horizon.

Even though he did his drills and learned to fold his gear in a sea bag at Basic, Martin was never going to set sail. He'd even tried to read the book, the *Bluejacket Manual*, to be a better sailor. It still got him no closer to the water. On that Monday in July, Martin had to wonder why he hadn't stayed home in Medina and gotten a job at A.I. Root or Permold.

Not a ship-shape sailor, Macky Martin worked as a warehouseman in the service of his country. Six days a week, he moved supplies, not ships. Freight came in on trains, and it was transferred to trucks, taken to the docks and then swung into the hold of cargo ships again and again in a never-ending cycle. As close to hoisting anchor as he'd ever get was watching the loads lifted over the side of the next outgoing freighter. The brass kept saying that it was essential, but that didn't keep it from being boring too. At least nobody could complain about the location though.

A sailor who got himself a forty-eight-hour pass had the world by the tail. Frisco was just an hour west. Sacramento had a lot going for it, too, off to the east. A thirsty man just had to go a few miles north into the Napa Valley and taste the grape. There was a lot to do on base as well, but it didn't seem to be really fighting a war to Macky Martin. It was duty though.

So, on that Monday, July 17, 1944, he got up, dressed, ate, saluted the lieutenant when he got his orders for the day and set to work. Another day moving freight. Taking crates off the train, across the yard and onto the loading platform again and again, waiting for eight hours to be over. Just another stateside, beach-bound sailor doing a day's work, never knowing that it was the last day of his life.

It would be called the "Port Chicago incident," one of the greatest maritime disasters of the war. The freight Martin and other sailors handled was ammunition. On this day, one shell slipped and went off. The chain reaction almost altered the course of the Pacific war.

The ammunition that was bound for the invasion forces at Saipan nearly went off with the force of an atomic bomb. More than three hundred were killed, five ships sunk at harbor and an entire train destroyed. Damage was reported seventy-five miles away. What remains miraculous is that this didn't happen all the time.

Safety standards as we know them today did not exist in 1944. Munitions were assembled in substandard production facilities and then carted by any available truck to a rail yard. Trains, although the most popular mode of transportation for all of society at the time, remained subject to derailment and collision on a regular basis. Dockworkers who may or may not have wanted to be there loaded supplies. Still, just once, only once, was the war effort slowed down because of such an accident.

They got on with the invasion at Saipan, the navy issued its reports and Port Chicago was rebuilt before the war in the Pacific ended. Life got back to normal, and most people forgot about some explosion somewhere out on the West Coast. Out there, far from Medina, where the hunt still goes on.

Seaman Alonzo Macky Martin, dockworker at the Port Chicago installation, still missing in the service of his country sixty-nine years later. Perhaps someday they will finally find something to bury. Gone but not forgotten, another one who never came home but lives forever with all the "Unknowns."

Part II

ABROAD

A WAR BEFORE THE WAR

May 3, 2012

We citizens of the United States tend to hold a high opinion of ourselves. Doing such, we forget that other nations might have been involved in winning World War II. Even filmmaker Ken Burns defines the conflict as the engagements between Pearl Harbor and a surrender ceremony on the battleship *Missouri*. Medina's Bill Brown had another view, a little more firsthand. By the time America would finally invade North Africa in November 1942, he'd already been under enemy fire for an entire year, and all he had to throw back was a crescent wrench.

Whether it was from a sense of adventure or a distaste of fascist principles, Brown had volunteered for duty with the American Field Service in November 1941. The AFS operated from 1920 to 1955, an alternative to active military duty for young men of the United States. By November 1941, that service was defined as being part of the ambulance corps in a place only slightly less dangerous than Pearl Harbor: the English front lines of North Africa.

It had started out as Italy's attempt at its greatest victory and turned into its greatest quagmire. An early defeat of spear-carrying Ethiopians gave confidence to the descendants of Caesar. Confronting the British, assorted elements of Free France and desert tribes bound by whoever had paid them last, the Italians received a huge dose of humility. To their rescue came their Axis partner, and in the sands of North Africa, reputations were made.

North Africa was the real estate where field marshals would claim rank. For the British, it was Wavell, Auchinleck and then a modest man named Montgomery, and the Germans would elevate a fox named Rommel. It was ground where military forces became immortal, the British 8th Army, its SAS and the Germans' Afrika Korps legendary to this day. It was history in the making, and Bill Brown of Medina saw it all.

Back and forth, two armies waged total war across the only passable ground—a narrow strip near the sea. The Italians were eliminated as a factor, but the Germans had moved east and then pushed back that early spring of 1942. As Bill Brown wrote home to Medina, it all was sunny skies and easy living, as his assignment was now with the Aussie boys near the Syrian border. He was a master mechanic, keeping the vehicles running on a front that seemed to be running down, in a war sure to be won at any time. At least that's what he told the folks, but he somehow forgot to mention it to the Germans.

Thirty-three thousand Brits were about to find out for themselves about the hardship of war. As Brown wrote of boar hunting with the mates from Down Under, Rommel and the Afrika Korps were moving east again, capturing the entire garrison at Tobruk. They would come within sixty miles of winning World War II this time. In the master plan of the "master race," capturing all of North Africa was all about oil and homeland security. Under Montgomery, the British lion would roar back from the edge of disaster, six months later joined by the Americans from the west, and within a year, the Afrika Korps would cease to exist. About then, Medina's own Brown was off to one more adventure.

As master mechanic of the American Field Service, Brown had sampled the good life, and he'd seen the terror of war, all within a few weeks in North Africa. He saw what an ambulance was for as the casualties came back from the front, and then he ducked for cover when he almost became a casualty to German artillery himself. When his next assignment came, it seemed too good to be true. In the stroke of a pen, he was off to that mysterious place called India. At least there it was sure to be a lot quieter than the English front of North Africa.

India, the staging grounds for units forever immortalized as the Chindits and Merrill's Marauders, two of the most savage jungle combat units ever created. India, the supply depot for the fight in Burma, China and all of Southeast Asia on land, sea and through the air. India, the backdoor to the most ruthless war fought in American history, the Pacific Theater, and master mechanic Brown saw it all too.

Bill Brown, in war before the rest of the nation knew what war was all about, but they were about to find out very, very quickly.

A Safe Assignment

May 24, 2012

Seville's Don Freese couldn't believe his luck that spring of 1942. It was the best of times for a navy swabie, at least this assignment. They called it a "milk run in paradise," sitting at his deck gun babysitting the tanker he was on. The war was going to be fought with him joyriding from New Orleans to Brazil and then back again transporting oil. Seaman Freese knew that these were the happy times of life. He just didn't know that one day in April, nine hundred yards away, another sailor was having the exact same thought.

His name was Harro Schacht, but the rest of the crew of German U-boat *507* called him "Kapitan." He thought it was the happiest of times, too, as he watched Seaman Freese's freighter through his periscope, lining up one parting shot before he sailed on to greener waters. If these Americans continued to be as stupid as they had been the first few months of the war, Korvettenkapitan Schacht would be home to stay in Hamburg long before Christmas.

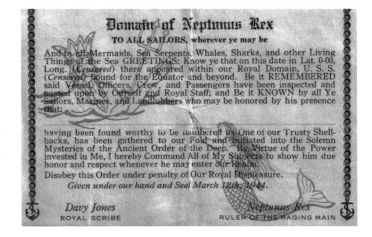

The reward for every sailor's first crossing of the equator, a shellback now and forever. *Diane Bumba Collection.*

Domain of Neptunus Rex

TO ALL SAILORS, wherever ye may be

And to all Mermaids, Sea Serpents, Whales, Sharks, and other Living Things of the Sea GREETINGS: Know ye that on this date in Lat. 0-00, Long. (*Censored*) there appeared within our Royal Domain, U. S. S. (*Censored*) bound for the Equator and beyond. Be it REMEMBERED said Vessel, Officers, Crew, and Passengers have been inspected and passed upon by Ourself and Royal Staff; and Be it KNOWN by all Ye Sailors, Marines, and Landlubbers who may be honored by his presence that:

having been found worthy to be numbered as One of our Trusty Shellbacks, has been gathered to our Fold and initiated into the Solemn Mysteries of the Ancient Order of the Deep. By Virtue of the Power invested in Me, I hereby Command All of My Subjects to show him due honor and respect whenever he may enter our Realm. Disobey this Order under penalty of Our Royal Displeasure.

Given under our hand and Seal March 12th, 1944.

Davy Jones
ROYAL SCRIBE

Neptunus Rex
RULER OF THE RAGING MAIN

In the greatest blunder of American military history, the government of the United States consigned hundreds of sailors to their deaths in the first year of the war through total ignorance. The nation had absolutely no comprehension of submarine warfare and its capability to bring it literally to the shores of the United States. The year 1942 ended being the one when America learned, and learned the hard way.

From sub pens in occupied France and Kiel, the Germans sailed to wage war in the Atlantic and then on the American coast. They had been in battle two full years, conditioned to life in conflict. The U-boaters came across the ocean that spring, beating the drum of the Fatherland, totally expecting total war. What they got was a welcome to the bright world of the most naïve United States.

By the lights of the Statue of Liberty, the U-boaters set their course. They listened to American radio as they stalked their prey, stunned that nowhere along the entire coast of the United States was there a blackout. It was the Happy Times for the Germans, ship after ship silhouetted by lights from shore into the perfect target. It was a time Harro Schacht knew very, very well.

It was on the second war patrol that the *U-507* found its hunting ground, the lights ringing the Gulf of Mexico assisting the Germans in sending nine ships to the bottom of the sea. More than ninety-one thousand tons of commerce was lost, but not the ship guarded by Seville's Don Freese. It was a lucky day for the Americans, with Kapitan Schacht on his way back to Lorient in France to resupply, the single torpedo he fired really just an afterthought of battle. It hit the Freese ship and did serious damage but didn't sink it. The U-boat would sail away, the lives of two men altered forever.

Kapitan Schacht would sail twice more from the pens in France, but he was not the same careful, cunning commander as the one who ravaged the Gulf in the spring of 1942. In the arrogance of the unbeatable, his next voyage would create an international incident when he sank ships of neutral Brazil within its territorial waters, drawing that nation into the war on the side of the Allies. On his next voyage, having just been decorated with the Knight's Cross, Kapitan Schacht and his crew would join the majority of their fellow U-boaters.

Forty thousand German sailors left port as submariners in World War II. Thirty thousand never saw home again, the most catastrophic loss of life in any branch of the service during the war. It only took one mistake, made on January 13, 1943, to be caught on the surface, the career and the lives of the men on the *U-507* ended by depth charges from a U.S. flying boat near the

Brazilian coast. Somewhere, one thousand miles away at that same moment in the Gulf, Seville's Don Freese was on duty at his gun.

There were no more milk runs, no more easy trips for any crewman once torpedoed. He had come home on leave, was given his fifteen minutes of fame as the war hero he was and went back to sea. No torpedoes would ever again hit his ship, but he'd never sleep easy as long as he was afloat. No salt would ever take life for granted again, but neither would one local boy and the kids he was about to teach.

THE AMERICAN HERO OF LODI

May 31, 2012

Americans have a limited ability to comprehend heroism. An excess of bravery jades the nation, allowing the outstanding to be eventually accepted with casual indifference. Just another citizen who happened to alter the course of history. That is a harsh opinion, but it's the only justification possible. That we grew tired of those we admired is the only rationale to explain why there aren't two statues to Dick Rowland on the Lodi town square.

Two tributes would be necessary for the man who made one immortal contribution to the winning of World War II and then branched out to make another. He achieved success for others and changed theaters, putting theory into practice, and then made even more difference in the outcome himself. He never considered himself a hero; he was just another flyer doing the jobs assigned. When the final surrender came, Dick Rowland was really just beginning. It would take nearly seventy years to realize how great one man could be.

The locals of Lodi knew that the postmaster's son was going to be a success even when he was still just a kid. Instead of hanging around the Idol Theater, he was in the library improving his mind. Achievement in academics continued to come after high school, first at Ohio State and then the University of Maryland, fine schools that could have led to a career as a marvelous engineer, but Dick Rowland wanted something else out of life that a man couldn't find in books. He could only get what he wanted in the sky. In 1938, Lodi's native son decided that he was destined to be a U.S. Army pilot.

First at Randolph and then Kelly Field, he learned the craft initially in antiquated biplanes and then basic trainers. Slowly the young aviator advanced through rank, the frivolity of youth occasionally irritating to some of the higher brass. By the time Dick Rowland picked up his major's cluster, he'd managed to antagonize some one-star enough to draw the worst assignment a pilot could find. Not just an instructor, Major Rowland was put in charge of teaching kids the army knew had no skill at a forgotten base—an airfield in some place called Tuskegee, Alabama. What the skinny kid from Lodi did was create legend.

They would eventually be known as the Red Tails, an elite fighter group that flew escorts to B-17s over Italy. These black pilots and aircrews had fought segregation and discrimination just to get the right to try to be soldiers and were now fighting the Germans with deadly effect. Major Rowland had trained the Tuskegee Airmen well, the unit winning countless awards and deserving even more by the time the war had ended, but the good major never got to see them in action. His job had been to give them necessary skills and send them off. He had his own date with fame just ahead.

Those who can, do. Those who teach, do it better. Seeing his protégés head to Europe, Major Dick Rowland volunteered for combat himself, not

Out to hunt the Japanese by air at a place called Bouganville. *Diane Bumba Collection.*

content with stateside life. It wasn't about glory or proving ability. Rowland was one of the 99 percenters of World War II Americans, well understanding duty and an obligation to a nation and accepting the true cost of freedom. He transferred to the 348th Fighter Group of Providence, Rhode Island, a unit soon to be on the move. The next stop would be New Guinea, South Pacific, and a date with some Zeros.

Rank and results gained privilege for Major Rowland, his chariot into battle being the state-of-the-art P-47Ds. At four hundred miles per hour from thirty thousand feet, the eight-machine-gun merchant of death had every advantage in the hand of a skilled pilot. As the skills and equipment of the Imperial Empire of Japan diminished in 1943 and 1944, American air supremacy grew by the hour. By the time the war ended, the instructor who had created the aces of the Tuskegee Airmen was an ace himself, eight Japanese flags painted on the side of a plane named the *Pride of Lodi, Ohio*. It was a marvelous military career that really had just begun.

Dick Rowland stayed with the military for another twenty-three years, rising to the rank of major general. He would work at the Pentagon, with Strategic Air Command and the CIA during the Cold War, ending his career as the chief of staff, Tactical Air Command, U.S. Air Force. Just another big brass who made good, even as another's luck was about to run out.

ON THE ISLE OF SAIPAN

June 21, 2012

Twenty-one beachheads had taught Lee more than just how to be a good Marine. On that sixteenth of June in 1944, he knew one basic fact: only a fool would want to be an officer. It wasn't telling teenage kids to go out and die; that wasn't the issue. It was what came next: sitting down and writing home to somebody's mother to tell her what a brave boy her son had been. Captain wasn't going to have it easy on the inferno they called Saipan. Eye-Tie didn't make it.

Eye-Tie was the nickname the guys had given the resident Italian of the outfit, Santo Doccolo. Dark hair, dark eyes and he could even speak the lingo, not that the Romance language had much use in the South Pacific. He was just a kid, a real kid, only nineteen when he got it doing his duty. Captain definitely would have it hard with this one, with everybody liking the boy. It was sure to be a painful letter back to his mother in some place called Wadsworth, Ohio.

There wasn't a man in the company, probably in the entire regiment, who didn't know Doccolo by the time the LST's opened up their doors at Saipan. He was a character, laughing any time there wasn't any shooting going on. Not that there'd been a whole lot of silence over the past eighteen months. Doccolo saw the good in everything, but he was one squared-away Marine too. Anybody who had any doubt just had to think back to Tarawa.

That had been the November before, the brass figuring there wouldn't be a whole lot to some little dot in the Marshall Islands. The Japanese had other ideas once the Marines had crossed the coral reefs. A lot more good boys died there than in North Africa before it was over. Only three, just three, out of five thousand Japanese survived, and Eye-Tie had done his share.

He and his squad had taken out thirty-four of the enemy in one attack. Doccolo had claimed that he got an admiral in charge, and that made the boys laugh. Old Eye-Tie didn't know the difference between a major and an admiral. At least he proved to be a good American—first thing when the shooting stopped, Doccolo started picking up some souvenirs to send back home. A first-class American even if some of his family couldn't quite claim the same.

It was the worst-kept secret of the Marine Corps, that Eye-Tie had some family on the other side. The boys in the outfit teased the Wadsworth kid unmercifully. While he was fighting the forces of the Rising Sun, his uncle was lounging in a POW camp somewhere in the States. As Doccolo ducked bullets, the uncle was getting three squares and a cot for the duration, his reward for being an Italian cavalryman with sense enough to surrender to the Americans in North Africa. The guys had always told Santo Doccolo that there was no justice for a squared-away Marine on this earth. Saipan would prove that far too true.

From June 16 to July 9 of 1944, three divisions of American forces would battle the fanatics of the Imperial Japanese Army for this piece of real estate. It was total war, no quarter asked or given in the relentless march to Tokyo for the Allies. The battle for Saipan was also the single most catastrophic engagement of the war for the boys from Medina, with more killed and wounded here than anywhere else in either theater. Thousands of soldiers on both sides never saw home again. Most never even saw what hit them.

Lee never wrote or said if he saw one of Wadsworth's best guys take his last breath. He only heard later that Eye-Tie wasn't coming home. Lee had problems of his own, lucky to have survived. Saipan would be Lee's last engagement, so badly wounded that he would spend the rest of his life on 100 percent disability, leaving that letter home to Mrs. Doccolo to the captain. A twenty-year-old kid like Lee didn't need things like that. It was going to be more important to try to make a living.

That he did, although most of the work was sporadic. Sometimes months at a time between jobs. Life ended up all right, though, gold statue or not. The tough Marine Lee, Lee Marvin, buddy to a guy who never got home to little old Medina County, USA.

CHASING THE WEATHER

July 12, 2012

She is the queen of the high-pressure system and tropical depression, the eternally radiant Betsy Kling. Each evening, she comes into northern Ohio homes via our television to make sense out of the weather. The Copley native who saw duty in Fort Wayne and Jacksonville can make an approaching tornado almost pleasant while still doing hundreds of hours of charitable works each year. Perhaps some day our own Betsy Kling will discover that she is just carrying on an old Medina County tradition.

It was back in the 1930s when Bill McQuistion first realized that he was a weather kind of guy. The local boy knew that there was just something about cloud patterns and precipitation that had much more of his interest than an afternoon of playing baseball. He liked the science of it, but he loved the speculation even more. Even then, the nuances of Medina County weather could be quite mysterious. Then, just as now, every day was a new adventure.

Making sense of tomorrow's forecast is the world's most inexact science. For all our technology today, for all our ability to look at the world from far above, Mother Nature continues to reign supreme. A most obvious frontal boundary of heavy rains five hundred miles to our west can be diverted or even dissolved by a thousand different factors before even reaching Ohio. Today, weather prognostication is a world of most likely occurrences. Once upon a time, it was more like a matter of the worst guess.

The National Weather Service was born out of the U.S. Army Signal Corps just after the American Civil War. The boys who once communicated by dots, dashes and signal flags became collectors of information from military posts nationwide. Temperatures and precipitations were reported and recorded, and trends were studied. The west–east pattern of prevailing winds was confirmed and the northwesterly flow of hurricanes and southeastern path of an Arctic clipper begun to be understood. Prediction was a hobby, though, the data collection being the real point of this branch of service. Data and its scientific facts that continue to be misunderstood today.

Perhaps we are indeed in the middle of global warming, but then again, it could well be an outset of the ice age as well. Fourteen decades of data as a sample over millions of years of existence isn't quite the survey size I recall being required in Statistics 401. Our priorities on numbers and not comprehension all those years from the 1870s had another effect on meteorologists back in 1943. Bill McQuistion really was working in the weather Stone Age.

Each day, he'd come to work at the office in England, seven days on duty and no days off. Such was army life in World War II. He'd gotten through Basic, but there wasn't much call for drill or rifle practice where he worked. There weren't even inspections, just a higher brass who always needed results. McQuistion's military duty was to read reports and make sense of it all. Every hour, reading another report from some weather station somewhere or a weather ship someplace. No satellites, no weather radar, just reports like they'd done it seventy years before. More information to plot on a map and hope he got it right. After all, the boys were counting on him.

Thousands of boys, just children, rising out of their bunks before dawn's early light each day, waiting to see what the fortunes of war were about to bring them. All across England they rose, sipped their coffee and then they waited for the news that only McQuistion could provide. Each morning for a few moments, Medina County's son was the most important man on earth. The boys all pinned their faith on an officer they'd never meet. Hoping he'd got it right, hoping there would always be a tomorrow in the violent world in which they lived in 1943. A world that we today will never understand.

In those rare moments when Betsy of the television gets the forecast wrong, we alter our plans for a few hours. Instead of a picnic, it's something indoors or the like. When forecaster Bill McQuistion got it wrong in 1943, it altered lives forever, even at fifteen thousand feet. Instead of Aachen, it would be Berlin that day. It was all up to Bill.

The weather guy of 1943 and meteorologist of the United States 8th Army Air Corps, the most famous fliers of World War II, Bill McQuistion of Medina County, USA.

The Young Salt of Wadsworth

July 26, 2012

Boot camp was tough, but nothing like playing football for the Grizzlies in the 1942 season. Wadsworth's Jack Trew knew that to be scientific fact. A new recruit at Great Lakes got pushed around a little bit, but nothing like the night they'd played Medina. That was a rough one, but Basic was different; it had a purpose beyond a scoreboard or bragging rights. There wasn't anything about a game in this. It was all about getting to be one squared-away seaman and getting after those Japanese.

From what Trew could tell from the newspapers, the war was already starting to turn against Tojo and his minions that spring of 1943. The Rising Sun had gotten its tail kicked at Midway, and scuttlebutt said it was just the beginning. Doing his share was what made Jack Trew show up at a recruiting office and get himself involved. He wasn't going to wait for a call from the Draft; he wanted to mix it up with the Pearl Harbor murderers. He got the right paperwork turned in, passed a couple of tests and was on his way just a few weeks later. Just another kid from Medina County, Ohio, about to be a most unusual hero.

There was more to the sailor Trew than the fact that he was one of the more outstanding recruits at Great Lakes. The record was clear: he did his drill well, he kept his gear stowed, he paid attention in class and the Shore Patrol had no reason to make his acquaintance on liberty. A quiet kid, not much of a gambler, but the other guys in his unit thought that he was all right for a country rube. A pretty good sailor even if his first assignment wasn't what a war hero had in mind.

Instead of firing salvos off the batteries of his nearest destroyer, Seaman Jack Trew was off tying bowlines for a rust bucket that the navy called a transport. They weren't exactly island girls standing at the dock to welcome the Yankee sailor either—more like Eskimos (the great disadvantage of ferrying supplies and troops to the place they called the Alaska Territory in 1943). It was orders, it was duty and better days were right around the corner. All Seaman Trew had to do was keep from blowing himself up.

It was the disadvantage of the Wadsworth salt's next duty station, an able-bodied seaman aboard a minesweeper. At least it was in the South Pacific, where the weather was warm. Nearly as warm as the action all around him. If the explosive devices they were clearing didn't blow the ship up, there were always the Japanese pilots who would be happy to oblige. If not them,

A little touch of home at Great Lakes Naval Recruiting Station, the newspaper to read and a football team that could beat Notre Dame. *Diane Bumba Collection.*

the Japanese destroyers. If not them, the Japanese submarines. Seaman Jack Trew learned fast that war is a twenty-four-hour-a-day proposition, but it was duty. It was orders, and the ship knew that it had one very good sailor in this kid named Trew.

The berth was in order, any order obeyed and Trew didn't even exercise his inherent right to complain. Not a peep about the skipper, the moronic ensign, not even the food. Seaman Jack Trew kept doing his job and doing it well. Out of a 4.0 scale, Trew graded out at 3.9, just about the finest enlisted man the U.S. Navy ever had. The skipper wasn't surprised shortly after when Jack Trew attracted the personal attention of the secretary of the navy. Unfortunately for Seaman Trew and his ship, it was for all the wrong reasons.

World War II inspired patriotism in this nation like never before and never since. Almost every American citizen found a way to become involved and aid the effort to end some of humanity's worst evils. For every trooper, there were ten on the homefront working toward the objective of victory.

As a people, we went above and beyond. For Jack Trew, it was a matter of being just a little bit early.

Three weeks after the secretary contacted the ship, Seaman Jack Trew was back in Wadsworth, honorably discharged for the moment. Nobody ever admitted who spilled the beans, not that it mattered. The old salt could get another chance someday, if the war lasted that long. If it lasted another two years, Jack would finally be old enough to enlist. Too young to serve, already having fought, just another of the amazing characters of the American fabric in World War II.

THE SUPER'S SON

August 2, 2012

He is the stuff that Hollywood movies were once made of, gritty films like *Battleground* or *The Story of G.I. Joe*. In 1943, he was just another senior at Medina High. By 1945, he was an aging, battle-scarred veteran, one of the Greatest Generation who served his time in hell. Today, he is the resident senior sage of Webster, New York, just another American hero, Private Craig Fenn.

Without World War II, he would have been just another fellow whose father was the superintendent of Medina Schools. They eventually named a school for his dad but, two generations later, pretty well forgot the facts of a good man's life. Fenn Road, an honor for the family, today more the Medina bypass instead of a tribute. It doesn't really matter to Private Fenn now. He's far too busy being modest.

The soft-spoken gentleman on the other end of the phone line gave me some argument about this concept of him being a hero. Like every veteran worth his salt, there was always somebody else from around here who had done more. The private's contribution wasn't that much, at least by his own account. To one of the State of Ohio's Distinguished Scholars of History, the facts said something completely different.

He was an eighteen-year-old kid that November 1943 in Basic at Fort Benning, Georgia, just another private in the ranks. Pneumonia put training behind schedule at first, and a brush or two with the brass didn't instill total military obedience, but the young man did grow as advanced training at Fort Jackson, South Carolina, came to an end. The order to ship overseas had come, and Private Craig Fenn did what many have done but never admit why. He went and got a picture taken for the folks in case he didn't make it back. He never dreamed how he almost wouldn't.

Craig Fenn was a dogface, the traditional ground-pounding, mud-slogging United States infantryman of World War II. He didn't make decisions; he just followed the guy ahead of him. The private didn't hang out with generals. He stayed glad that the sergeant didn't yell at him too much. He learned how to shave without water and that his helmet made a lousy toilet by the time his outfit walked the perimeter around camp in France. He learned all that and that he was a lucky trooper. Craig Fenn didn't step on the German land mine, but the guy behind him did.

It was a ten-dollar wound, not one of those million-dollar ones that got a kid shipped home. Most guys hit where Fenn was struck ended up with a limp for life; he just got his first claim to a Purple Heart, wounded in action. To the Medina school super's son, it wasn't that much, no battle at all. It gave him a little time off, and then it was back with the unit, back to wherever it was the action was supposed to be. The Germans made sure Private Craig Fenn knew exactly where that was: right on top of him.

Odd as it might seem to a television generation, dogface ground-pounding infantrymen really don't know that battle has begun until some time after it's over. Moving through woods the Germans just left seems so easy in a movie. In real life, when the Germans had already zeroed in their artillery on the grounds they just left, it's a quick look into the jaws of hell where all that mattered was staying alive. There is no plan, and there is no line to maintain; there's only cover to find and then to pray, knowing there is a God after all.

There had to be after one mortar barrage, with Craig Fenn's second claim to the Purple Heart stopped by the steel-backed Bible he carried in his left front jacket pocket. His mother had given it to him for reading when he'd left home, with nobody dreaming what salvation there was in the Salvation. A dogface considered himself lucky, even as that luck was running out.

It was just another patrol, with the Germans pulling back. Just carry the maps and follow the guy ahead, and let the Sarge do the talking—that was Private Fenn's duty. If it got crazy, he did have his grease gun, and then it got too quiet, way too quiet. The super's son ended up with his third claim to a Purple Heart, with a German's machine pistol pointed at his head a long way from that thing called freedom.

The Prisoner Fenn

August 9, 2012

It was the farce of all farcical television comedies in the 1960s, the CBS production known as *Hogan's Heroes*. Somehow, life inside a prisoner of war compound in Germany during World War II became amusing each week. We tuned in to watch brilliant Allies and dimwitted Germans inside the wire at Stalag 13C outside of Hammelburg. Too bad nobody asked Medina's Craig Fenn about it. After all, he was there.

Stalag 13C was the last stop in the life of World War II captivity for the son of Medina's school superintendent. What had started out as a routine patrol as the war was winding down ended up with Fenn wounded in action, his buddies disappeared and a German standing over him pointing a pistol at the American private's head. What happened next was nothing like we saw or even see today on the sacred idol of TV.

Today, we carry a History Channel image of the German army shooting prisoners, inflicting savage cruelty and ruthlessly campaigning wherever they went. For Prisoner Fenn, it was a world where his captors were well aware that the war was ending and they were losing. The Germans were on the move to avoid capture themselves, with Allied forces closing in on all sides. They knew that there would be retribution for what had happened in the previous six years, with Craig Fenn's captors making the best of a bad situation. It was almost like he was one of them.

A German medic and then doctor treated his gunshot wound, making sure the American private got the spent slug as a souvenir. German guards shared a beer ration with the recently captured Amis on what seemed like an endless train ride to nowhere. More guards made sure German civilians kept their distance from the enemy who had just bombed their houses. The Americans were fed as best could be, with the Germans speaking English as much as possible to what they hoped would soon be their own captors. Much better than if the Russians got there first.

Private Fenn had never seen any of those so-called Allies the Russians before his long and winding road finally stopped at Stalag 13C. One glance and he understood instantly what had been the Eastern Front of no quarter asked or given. The British and American prisoners had rations, but the Soviets would eat grass. They watched the West forlornly from their own compound, hated by the Germans and despised by their own government for having given up. It was a world without hope that was reborn without so much as a goodbye. With the dawn one morning, the Germans were just gone.

It was only a matter of a few hours before the American military broke down the wire around the camp and sent the prisoners on their way. There was still a war to win, no time to take care of former captives other than to point them to the rear. Although he would never fire a rifle in anger again, Craig Fenn still had some war to see before he made it home.

He'd seen the V-2 rockets launched, what would become the American space program one day used as a supersonic merchant of death to thousands of English civilians during the war. Now on his walk to the rear, he saw what seemed like the entire Hungarian army in captivity, once a German partner, now just a mass of oddly uniformed men waiting to go home, if home was still there. He saw the German Me262, the first combat jet, in action overhead, too fast to be caught by American fighters and too late to make a difference. Finally, after too many miles and hitched rides, he finally saw the light at the end of the tunnel.

The German surrender was signed as Craig Fenn was somewhere in the middle of the Atlantic Ocean truly headed home. Just about all he carried along with him on the SS *George Washington* was a spent bullet, a pocketknife and a lot of memories. They made port in New York as if they were immigrants from a half century before, a world of desolation behind them and a new life awaiting. A new life and a new nation we've almost let slip away.

Craig Fenn was not a Medal of Honor recipient or a Silver Star winner. He is simply an American hero, soldier and citizen duty bound, just like a neighbor, a kid from down the road who went off to sail the seas and did end up being somebody quite special.

AN ADMIRAL A LONG WAY FROM HOME

October 4, 2012

Japanese Vice Admiral Jisaburo Ozawa knew that the world was in the palm of his hand that May 1944. The glory that had escaped him in the first three years of the war was now stretched out before him, waiting to be claimed. As he studied the maps in his headquarters in Borneo, it was obvious to the most casual observer that the Americans were ripe for the picking. Vice Admiral Ozawa was not a casual observer; he was a man on a mission.

He had paid his dues, of that there was no doubt. A graduate of the Japanese Naval Academy. Trained in cruiser and destroyer command. Chief of staff to this admiral or that. He had taken a command when the war with the Americans began, but all eyes had been on Pearl Harbor. No one had noticed his brilliance in the Dutch East Indies. Now would be different, though, and the world would see; Vice Admiral Ozawa was about to win the war.

His two fleets would sail north, the Americans totally distracted by their invasion of Saipan. They would never see his carriers until the planes had already launched, too late for the Americans to divert. Twenty-five Japanese submarines would ring the invaders, isolating their carriers first and then their heavier battleships. The Philippine Sea would soon be lined with American steel hulls. Admiral Ozawa couldn't help but smile as he issued his orders to sail, never knowing that across the water to the east, Joe was smiling too.

Lieutenant Joe Rochefort sat in his office, clad in his favorite bathrobe, feet propped up on his desk, and watched the teletype machine as it clattered away. Since September 1940, he'd be able to decode most of the Japanese radio messages, but not all. He'd known that something was up before Pearl Harbor, but not specifics. He'd gotten Midway right, though, right on the money. Now Ozawa seemed to be up to something, audaciously sending two fleets to the Philippine Sea. Lieutenant Rochefort sent the messages along, hoping that the new commander would have enough sense to read them and understand that the code-breakers had gotten this one right too.

This Vice Admiral John Hoover was supposed to be a good man, but he'd spent the first two years of the war in the Atlantic. That was a different theater, the only threat being the German U-boats. The Pacific was different. The ocean was a three-dimensional battlefield every second of every day. Rochefort had never met the commander, and the best he could do was hope that the Old Man had the sense he was supposed to have and would do the right thing. On the morning of June 19, 1944, Rochefort and the rest of the world discovered that Vice Admiral Hoover was smarter than they'd ever dreamed. The Japanese force was sailing into one of the greatest slaughters in the history of naval warfare.

Military histories would label the next forty-eight hours as the Battle of the Philippine Sea. To the American carrier pilots, it would always be remembered as the "Marianas Turkey Shoot." The undertrained and underequipped Japanese carrier pilots did manage to shoot down 29 American aircraft the first day of battle. In return, they lost 273 themselves, as well as two of their own carriers. The next day, another Japanese carrier and 65 more planes found their way to the bottom. For the Imperial submarines, it was even worse.

The Japanese submariners never got near their assigned positions before American destroyers were dropping depth charges on top of them. Seventeen of the twenty-five were sunk those two days, with the remainder engaged in escape rather than attack for the duration of the battle. It was a complete American victory, the Rising Sun now beginning its final setting just as one vice admiral began to fade into the obscure footnotes of history.

It was not Ozawa, though, who later commanded at Leyte Gulf and was remembered for his skill, but rather John Hoover, who would become the one rarely mentioned in history. Even though he remained in command, in charge at Iwo Jima, only the serious scholars of the conflict have heard the great man's name. Nimitz, Halsey and Spruance they know, but Hoover is almost forgotten. Perhaps that's because the great naval commander came from a place more famous for people even bigger to the point of being giants.

Indeed, Admiral John Hoover, commander, Forward Area of the Pacific, was born and raised in Seville, right here in little old Medina County, USA.

FIFTY TIMES A HERO

October 11, 2012

It is the definition of courage to once climb into a battle-bound B-17 and take a position as the ship's radio operator. It is the definition of an American hero to have done it fifty times six months before the landings at Normandy. Such were the life and times in 1943 of Wadsworth's Tom Gaertner.

Each morning of a mission, he would awaken early, a military breakfast and coffee not much of a sendoff to just another young man doing his duty. There would be a briefing, a final check of his own personal gear and then the ride out to the ship. One by one, they climbed in, each and every man well aware of the duty with which his nation had entrusted him. Each and every one wondered if that day, whatever the day might be, would be the last of the good luck.

It had been a long journey that brought the Sharon native to aerial combat in World War II, as an individual and as a unit. He was a member of the 99th Bomb Group, another example of the military's best of intentions but worst of plans. The unit had been organized on September 25, 1942, and activated in Boise, Idaho. Quickly realizing that learning to fly and fight in the harsh conditions of the Rockies might impede progress, the U.S. Army Air Corps soon transferred the 99th to Walla Walla, Washington. Just a few weeks of Pacific Northwest rain and fog had the unit on the move again, first to Iowa and finally to Salina, Kansas, by January 1943. Within ninety days, the conditions of training were long forgotten, and the world of combat was at hand.

Assigned to the 5th Bombardment Wing of the 12th Air Force, Tom Gaertner and the boys arrived in Marrakech, Morocco, via Florida, South America and then onto the continent of Africa heading north. By March 31, 1943, the 99th was in the air on its first mission in one of the more forgotten elements of World War II, at least to Americans. The men were out to destroy Germany's Afrika Korps one supply ship at a time.

Slowly but surely, the troops of Hitler were losing ground in North Africa, in the east as the British advanced and from the west after the American landing in Operation Torch the November before. Throughout it all, even as they had been advancing, the Germans were losing supplies on a daily basis. The British controlled the seas from their base at Malta, and they were gaining the advantage in the air as well. With the arrival of the Americans of the 99th Bomb Group, it became just a matter of time to African victory.

There were still battles to be fought and missions to be flown in the name of the cause. Each mission, Tom Gaertner would climb into the best of American engineering, the B-17, and take his place. Ahead of him in the ship, on the upper level, would sit the pilot and co-pilot, usually the old men of the crew, perhaps as ancient as twenty-five. Beneath them, the navigator and the bombardier—one to get them there, the other to make it worthwhile. Near Gaertner was the flight engineer, the master mechanic of all things on the ship. Behind him the belly gunner, two waist gunners and the tail gunner, out to make sure they all got home. For Wadsworth's Tom Gaertner, it was duty to make sure they didn't miss anything.

From his position as radio operator, Gaertner was responsible for relaying any messages from other ships or the ground up front. Some were in clean air, some were coded and all were important enough for him to record each in a log book as they flew to and from their assignment of the day. It was enough to keep any human busy as massed formations took wing, but this was combat as well. Working a radio was essential, but so, too, was Tom Gaertner's best friend each mission, his .50-caliber machine gun.

Fifty times he took flight, and fifty times he came back, the Wadsworth resident rewarded with the Air Medal and ten clusters as a souvenir. Too bad he didn't get to bring home that other achievement on his record: the Me109 that he put down somewhere in the Mediterranean.

Just another day's work in the life of yet another real American hero, Tom Gaertner, and yet there would be others even more courageous. The brave ones who not only didn't have a plane but also didn't even have a gun.

THE BIRTH OF THE EMT

October 25, 2012

Collectively, their name was Doc, but very few ever went to medical school before or after their time in hell had ended. With one target painted on

The angels of battle: the medics plying their trade somewhere in Europe in 1944, long before the rest of us came to rely on the EMTs. *National Archives and Records Administration, 208-YE-22.*

their helmet and another on their arm, working two to a company of one hundred troopers, they served the duration given a simple charge. All they had to do was locate a wounded trooper, apply immediate medical assistance and then transport the injured back to an aid station for treatment. That and stay alive.

Battlefield casualties have been an issue in every war America has ever fought, from the Revolution through the Barbary Coast and across the Civil War into the future today. It was not until the twentieth century, though, that science could be coupled with medicine—earlier physicians more often held basic educations that may or may not have included medical college. By 1941, the treatment of the potentially wounded had become all a matter of by-the-book regulation.

According to military dictum, every soldier in the field would carry a personal medical kit to include sulfa powder, two vials of morphine and bandages to handle the flesh wounds of the movies and keep on fighting. Two company medics would roam the battlefield assessing more serious wounds, calling in evacuations as necessary. From the field, the more seriously wounded would be transported by jeep back to Battalion Aid for a doctor's treatment. The most serious would then be transported by truck

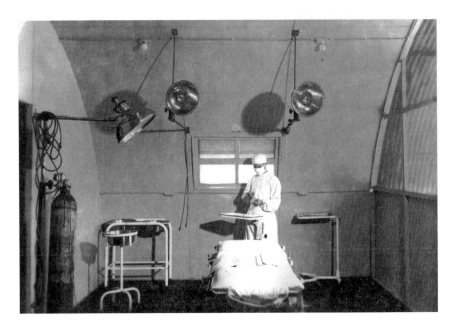

An operating room somewhere in the South Pacific. From appendicitis to shrapnel wounds, this was the ER of the war front all over. *Diane Bumba Collection.*

back to the regimental field hospital for the best of care. It was the perfect plan by the rules of war. Rules that, once shooting started, nobody seemed to have read.

Medics crossing a field were nothing but moving targets to opposing forces as battles raged. Columns of trucks clearly marked with a red cross within a white circle offered the same objective as a detachment of Sherman tanks to a Me109 five thousand feet above. Legion is the name of the number of artillery shells that fell on battalion and regimental hospitals located near military objectives. In theory unarmed noncombatants, medical personnel of the United States military themselves accounted for somewhere between 2 and 4 percent of the total casualties in the war. It was a world that Medina's Harvey Shiery and Charley Doljes knew quite well.

A most unhappy sailor, but there was a reason. One week after this picture was taken, the seaman first class almost died from the real killer of the Asian theater: malaria. *Sharon Beachy Collection.*

It was for the victims of the Japanese that they worked their magic, moving through the jungle of New Guinea one moment and treating a local villager's broken bones from being tortured by a withdrawing enemy the next. Throughout it all, a war raged twenty-four hours a day to the front, the flanks and the rear against an enemy not known for compassion. War in the midst of some of nature's most inhospitable grounds for medical care.

If it wasn't the heat, then it was the rain. If not the rain, the snakes, and if not the snakes, then there was the polluted water. Through it all, the Medina boys worked, slithering through the tall grass as Oriental bullets passed overhead. Constantly on edge, listening for the call and watching for the sign. The call, "Medic," or the rifle inverted into the ground with the helmet on the butt, not a sign of a grave but perhaps of the gravely wounded and enemy nearby. Through it all they worked, like thousands of their brothers in aid across the Pacific and in Europe. Each and every medic knew that for a corpsman, there were only two ways out: hero or dead.

For Sergeant Doljes, it would be the hero, one act of bravery leading to another on Bouganville, eventually being a key element of the 37th Division's Presidential Unit Citation for valor. For Doc Shiery, the only honor was the letter his folks got from his commander in New Guinea explaining how a good man had given his all in the name of his troops, another who never saw home again.

To the thousands of troops they saved, there would be one eternal thought, far more valuable than any cross of nickel or tin. To them, the grandfathers of those valiant who today ride in the EMTs who continually strive to make human life more sacred, there was one truth born in the battlefields all around the world. If a man was a combat trooper and didn't come home loving "Doc" until the day he died, he never was a combat trooper.

Great American heroes, the medics, but even they couldn't help one local boy when fate chose him to be first.

BAD TIME TO BE FIRST

November 1, 2012

Stan Vanselow never doubted the wisdom of being a Wilkie man in the 1940 election for president. The Great Depression hadn't really affected him, the concepts of WPA and soup lines were not much more than pictures in the newspaper to the Medina boy. Roosevelt had his positive points, but two terms had been good enough for Washington; it should have been good enough for a modern world too. It was time to let Wilkie and his running mate McNary take control, at least to one first-time voter.

That was back in the day when casting your first vote in a major election was a right of passage to adulthood in this country. You were a man or a woman at that moment, rendering a rational decision on what you read in the newspapers, heard on the radio and how your parents told you to vote. A first-time voter actually grinned when he'd show up at the polls, signed his name and then rendered his view via the ballot box, finally able to fulfill the greatest American right. The 1940 election didn't go quite the way young Vanselow thought it should, though. It almost made a novice Republican wonder if the nation would survive.

The war in Europe wasn't going to go away, the quiet from the time the Germans invaded Poland in '39 replaced by the conquest of France that summer of 1940. The Japanese were on the march in the Far East. It was just a matter of time before it involved the United States; Stan Vanselow of Grangerburg knew that as an absolute fact when he cast his ballot in November. By the next summer, he knew that there was only one thing he could do as an American adult. Stan Vanselow was off to enlist.

On July 9, 1941, Vanselow entered the ranks of the United States Army, another candidate for aviation training, his 20/20 vision a key ingredient to the place he wanted to be. It wasn't enough to just be in the air; Grangerburg's favorite son wanted that front-left seat and the title of pilot to go with his lieutenant's bars. He worked hard, and he got the assignment and even more. His first ship was the magnificent brand-new bird known as the B-24.

It was Consolidated Aircraft's finest effort of the war, the B-24 Liberator, the workhorse of all theaters of Allied operation. More than nineteen thousand would be constructed between November 1941, when it first went into service, and war's end. For Lieutenant Vanselow, there was no finer chariot of battle, capable of nearly three hundred miles per hour and willing to drop four tons of payload from twenty-eight thousand feet. It was the perfect plane until it all went wrong, and the boy from Grangerburg claimed the one distinction no one ever wanted.

Perhaps it was a broken hydraulic line, perhaps a wing sheared off, or maybe it was even pilot error; the cause was never determined. All that mattered was that during the third week of August in 1942, Lieutenant Vanselow's ship went down in the North African desert. There was no enemy action involved, with the military writing it off as just another accident, but there were no survivors, and Lieutenant W. Stan Vanselow became the first Medina County boy to die during the declared conflict to end oppression known as World War II.

Nearly 3,000 Medina County men and women served the military during World War II. More than 150 never came home. Of them, no more than one-third had ever cast a ballot in an election to determine the fate of a nation before they left to become men and women. They didn't have to be begged to go overseas to do their duty; they had a comprehension of that long before they put on their uniforms. It was all about doing the right thing, supporting the principles that had let them have the chance to live the way we all so take for granted today.

What a great tragedy it would be that it would become too inconvenient to cast a ballot, that our own ignorance or indifference would keep us at home on Election Day. Lieutenant Vanselow had one chance, and some had none at all, but their sacrifice ensured that we do. What a tribute to the Greatest Generation, that every citizen over eighteen turned out to vote, especially here in the place that gave so much, little old Medina County, USA.

THE FEEDING OF THE MASSES

November 22, 2012

The United States military would consider this its greatest challenge. The average dogface trooper thought that it was the greatest secret weapon the Germans and Japanese had in their arsenals. Historians today remain amazed at how it was even possible, the feeding of the millions of American troopers in World War II both home and abroad.

Today is Thanksgiving, the annual event when our relatives inflict themselves on us in the name of gratitude. At our house, the cats have formed up around the stove, waiting for the arrival of the giant robin as my B.W. whips potatoes into a frenzy. By three o'clock this afternoon, the felines will be assuming more human characteristics beside me, passed out from gluttony, and the plates will be bare. We will feed ten today. For the army cooks of World War II, it was more like ten thousand.

Ten thousand is a rough approximation of the size of an army division of combat troops. Just one division, three or more of which would make up a corps. Three corps make an army. Not *the* army, just one army of several under the Stars and Stripes. Thousands of troopers expecting turkey and potatoes and expecting them hot no matter where they were, no matter when it was, and that was just the army and its air corps. There was the navy and its Marines as well, millions of meals for thousands of days.

For a stationary army, feeding the masses is a difficult task but far from impossible. The Civil War truly created the concept of the field kitchen for combat troopers. By World War II, it was an art form of ovens where the quality of the food was directly related to the waistline of the cook. It was when the troops were on the move that chow at times would become a soldier's worst nightmare, and it was called the Rats. Not a rodent, though; Rats was short for rations, contained units of food to be eaten in the field under combat conditions. Today called Meals Ready to Eat (MREs), the Rats of World War II were categorized as C, D or K. Long before a president's

To the dogfaces, it was Germany's greatest secret weapon: an American chow line in the middle of winter in 1945. *National Archives and Records Administration, Newhouse Collection, 111-SC-198849.*

wife deemed it necessary to reform American eating habits, all three Rats filled daily nutritional needs. Whether or not it was edible was up to every dogface to decide.

It was the C-Ration that would become the most popular field feeding tool for the Americans during World War II. One day's requirements inside a cardboard box, stowed inside a knapsack. There would be three cans of meat and vegetables, three cans of crackers, coffee, sugar and candy. Armed with a can opener and a campfire, a trooper could survive, with every meal a new adventure. He could also console himself as he pried open a C-Rat lid that at least they weren't Ds.

The D-Ration—the real reason many dogfaces knew the enemy must have had something to do with the food planning of the military—was a variation on the Civil War tradition of hardtack. Instead of flour, water and salt baked beyond recognition, the D-Ration was a chocolate bar that was meant to be a substitute for a full meal. Weighing in at about six hundred calories per bar, it was a last resort of food, especially in the South Pacific; some claimed it had no purpose other than to justify the division dentist's position. About all a trooper could do was hope that there was some fool willing to trade a dozen Ds for just one K.

The K-Ration, originally designed for issue to all paratroopers, was a Holy Grail to many ground pounders of World War II. Three separate boxes, three separate meals, made up the daily issue. There were fortified biscuits, canned meats, malted milk tablets, bouillon packets, coffee, lemonade powder and even chewing gum in the day's meal. It wasn't home cooking—it wasn't even chow hall issue—but it was better than Cs or Ds. They were all edible but best forgotten once that war came to an end. When that war did end, the troopers rushed back home, never to complain of the wife's cooking again. None dreamed that they were only beginning a life with the next generation of Rats we call SpaghettiOs.

All that meat and vegetables packed in millions of cans, made in a factory owned by the one and only Chef Boyardee of Cleveland, Ohio, just up the road from little old Medina County, USA.

In the Matters of Faith

November 29, 2012

For Pastor Jim Gilbert of the Presbyterian faith, one minute he's preaching the Good Word, the next he's joining another committee in the name of good works. He might take a breath, but then he's off on visitation or sampling every item on the church social's potluck, just ensuring quality. A good man in a difficult occupation, but at least he's got it easier than his World War II contemporaries. Pastor Gilbert's only got to deal with one faith.

Things were different for the military chaplains in Europe and the Pacific during the war. It wasn't unusual for a padre to hit for the cycle in the course of his duties. More than one opened the day saying Mass before moving on to Episcopal dogma, Presbyterian theology, Methodist wisdom and Baptist belief, concluding with a few readings from the Torah to minister to the needs of his boys. All the while he preached wondering if the artillery overhead was outbound or incoming mail from a greater power. A very tough calling that was rewarded in a way soldiers knew best: they gave the chaplains a nickname.

Through it all, they kept their faith, even in a place called Normandy. *National Archives and Records Administration, Sergeant Steele Collection, 127-N-82262.*

They were the sky pilots, the ones who rode with God. No matter what his belief, every dogface admired the man of the cloth as he came around, into the lion's den, to live his conviction and share it with others. Chaplains jumped into Normandy with the Pathfinders and stormed the shores of Tarawa with the Marines, all the time carrying little more than a communion set in their kits. Brave men of God who had come to the front to confirm the obvious.

Everett Perkins, at his top turret position in a B-17 over Rabaul, understood it. So did Vance Grimes even before he was wounded up in the Aleutians. They and millions of others were able to comprehend the basic fact of war—the greatest incongruity of humanity seeking religion. Man is never more in touch with his God than when he looks into the jaws of earthly hell. For a soldier of World War II, every day was an encounter with Armageddon.

They saw on the shores of Anzio and at Normandy what Dante had once written about. The devil's playground truly was on hundreds of islands throughout the South Pacific. Lucifer himself rode the ack-ack over Aachen as it tried to find another target lumbering high overhead. Troopers saw it all and heard the angels sing as well when they survived in a lifetime that could last just minutes, knowing full well with the dawn that they would do it all over again.

A combat trooper who doubted the existence of God was never a combat trooper—that is a truth of all things military. There can be no other excuse for our own stupidity to engage in war than the expectation that there is some divine force overseeing it all, some power far beyond our own. Whether the Lord is protecting the good or punishing the wayward sinner, he was in every foxhole and every landing craft, every aid station and every airplane throughout World War II. Once the final battle had ended, he would stay with the Greatest Generation for years to come as well.

The postwar years saw the greatest increase in church attendance in the history of the United States. Every traditional faith grew in every community as GIs came home to sanity; there was no need to make religion convenient or alter the Gospel to make it acceptable to a social agenda in those days. The sky pilots and a damn war had done their jobs well, renewing man's faith to survive in this life and aspire to a better one in the next. Returning veterans had no doubt in his power. For one young veteran, it was even more.

He was never mentioned by name when he came back, at least not in the local papers or polite conversation, this combat veteran who had once hailed from Chatham. His situation was just too inconceivable to begin to report. No one knew what he had seen or what had happened while he was a soldier to make him the way he became. We barely understand posttraumatic stress today, let alone understood it then. It was all for the better that society just would let him be.

The combat veteran who spent the rest of his earthly life believing that he truly was Jesus Christ, the savior of mankind.

When Last Became First

December 6, 2012

He could be considered Medina County's last casualty of World War I, but that's just a technicality. Splitting hairs like that wasn't a high priority for Wadsworth's Horace Messam. After all, he hadn't even been born when the shooting stopped in the Great War. Politics and world affairs never held a lot of interest for the young man who grew up in the house on Route 224. He just wanted to be a good aircraft mechanic seventy-one years ago at a place called Pearl Harbor.

A war had been raging for two years in Europe by that Sunday morning in 1941. The armistice of November 11, 1918, and then the treaties that the United States had never approved were long forgotten. That was Europe, though, a situation to be watched. When it came to the Pacific, it was a crisis to be worried about.

The Empire of Japan had been on the march long before Hitler's Panzers rolled into Poland. The battles fought in the Far East were ruthless, a savagery almost unimaginable to Americans. The flag of the Rising Sun was on the move through China and then Southeast Asia. Military intelligence calculated the objective to be Australia; no doubt a war was coming. It was just a matter of when and where the Japanese would invade that continent. Military intelligence would never be more wrong.

Misunderstanding the Japanese was nothing new to the Western world. Blanket characterizations of any foreign power cast stereotypes and caricatures into the American mindset. When the first images of the war crimes the Japanese were capable of were seen, the West was horrified but not enough to actually act. That was all happening in China, not here. Eventually, there would be a war; that was common knowledge. Just not yet.

There were warning signs, but no one really noticed time and time and time again in the years and then months and then days before Pearl Harbor. At any rate, some veterans would later claim that Pearl was much better known for parties than preparedness in those halcyon times when one Oriental was off killing another. The facility was the jewel of all naval bases, set in paradise that was once known as the Sandwich Islands. It was a paradise that Sunday morning that turned into hell.

It was near seven o'clock that morning when the Rising Sun came in from the northwest. More than two thousand United States servicemen were within moments of their death, with some never even waking before a torpedo from a Nakajima Kate slammed into their ship. Horace Messam was up, bullets from a Zeke machine gun cutting him down as he ran for cover. Within just two hours, it was a complete Japanese victory. A victory that was, in fact, the beginning of their defeat.

Despite total surprise, the Japanese still lost twenty-seven planes and all of their midget submarines in the December 7 attack. They had missed the submarine pens at one end of the island and attacked totally oblivious to the fact that the United States aircraft carriers weren't at harbor but were out to sea. Within twenty-four hours, there was a declaration of war issued by the U.S. Congress. The Rising Sun had just awoken a sleeping giant as one Medina County boy closed his eyes for the last time.

The Japanese campaign for world domination continued, with the Philippines rapidly falling. Singapore soon came under the banner of the emperor followed by a tiny outpost called Wake Island, all within six months of the assault on Pearl Harbor—the six months it took the United States to become mobilized and ensure, after a place called Midway, that the Rising Sun was setting and would never win another battle of World War II.

Private First Class Horace Messam wasn't the county's first casualty of World War II. That war for the United States hadn't been declared until the next day, December 8, but that's just a technicality. Splitting hairs like that isn't a high priority for current historians. After all, we hadn't even been born when the shooting stopped in World War II. We do, however, have a habit of understanding what it all led to in the end.

A local boy, the first of the many. The noble men and women willing to pay the ultimate price, now dying out without even a national holiday to recall their sacrifices. Private Horace Messam, one of the many real American heroes in a way that had just begun.

THIS COMING SATURDAY

December 13, 2012

There was a light snow falling in Belgium sixty-eight years ago this coming Saturday. For one buck sergeant and his driver, it was just another miserable day. The snow was cold, the colonel had sent them out to see if anything was going on and now, as darkness approached, they were out of cigarettes. A bad day but sure to get better. Tanks were coming.

The war was almost over, and it was incredibly quiet for combat troops just then. No action, just waiting. Waiting like the sergeant and driver did as they pulled over to the side of the road to wait for the armor. They could always trade something for smokes. Around the corner they came, the Sarge maintaining that they were the biggest pieces of machinery he'd ever seen. Solid black in color, no markings, just the commander of the lead tank visible as he sat on top of the turret wearing a T-shirt and his headset. The commander saw the jeep, straightened up and gave a salute as the armor rolled past.

It took a minute, but the question did come from the jeep driver as to why they hadn't stopped those boys to trade. The non-com posed a question in return: when exactly is a sergeant saluted in the American army. The driver finally grasping the correct answer (that he's not), the jeep rocketed back to headquarters to report the situation to Military Intelligence, which laughed off the ridiculous story of a sergeant and his driver. They were told to go sleep it off, to forget it and not bother anybody again.

That they did, at least until about six o'clock the next morning, when the wake-up call was the barrage of German 88mm artillery. In a panic, the order was given to fall back, the troopers scrambling to get out of town as fast as possible. Gear was thrown onto trucks, troopers were running and total chaos ruled the day. For that sergeant, there was just enough time for one last goodbye to his sweetheart.

She was just a little Belgian girl, maybe eight, maybe not, whom he'd seen every day with her father. He'd give her chocolates and try to make conversation, but about all the two locals would do was smile in return. In the two weeks he'd been in town, all he'd managed to understand was that the little angel's name was Maria. The sergeant saw his girl, jogged over to pass out the last of his chocolate and get one more smile. Instead, he got the surprise of his life.

"Those were King Tigers you saw yesterday," the local man said. "They are SS, they are the Blowtorch Battalion, they are murderers and they headed right here, Sergeant. You must stop them."

It was one of those moments of total understanding that come to humans so rarely; the sergeant stared just a few seconds before he said, "Resistance?"

"Now you know it. The Germans know it too. You must stop them."

History would eventually record the next thirty days of the war as the Battle of the Bulge. To one buck sergeant, it was a month of walking on the edge of the abyss. He would win a Bronze Star at a fuel dump in Stavelot, burning gas as the German armor came up the road. He was just outside Malmedy watching as his unit brushed the snow away from the bodies of murdered American prisoners of war. Through the insanity of war and winter, he trudged on, not as the victor but rather just another survivor. When it all got quiet, with the Germans retreating, he went back looking for his little friend. She and her father were gone, not one of the locals remembering the two strangers who came to town the day before the Americans arrived.

Over the next fifty years, the sergeant went back to Belgium twice as the average tourist. He never did find Maria to give her one last chocolate—just the places he'd been. The second trip he even found the bend in the road where he had once rated a German salute. Until the day he died, he maintained that that twist of pavement had made him grateful for life every day after.

A good life after the war, happily married to his sweetheart, raising one great daughter and one average son. A typical American just glad to have survived.

THE YEAR OF A GOOD CHRISTMAS

December 27, 2012

It was the best Christmas gift John C. Murray could have gotten, even better than the bottle of hooch and the box of cigars the Old Man left on his desk. It was even better than being back home in Chippewa Lake, at least

Luxury living in the South Pacific. *Diane Bumba Collection.*

for the moment. The other guys could go walk on the beach and ogle the Aussie girls—Murray would just sit with his feet propped up and savor that Christmas Day in 1942. He was alive. He'd survived Guadalcanal.

For three months, he'd been a part of what the Pearl Harbor brass had labeled Operation Watchtower. That brass had never seen the stink hole of an island other than on a map or in a picture from high above. It was all part of the grand master plan, taking the Pacific back from the Japanese. The Rising Sun had begun to set at Midway, but it was a long road to Tokyo. It would be an even longer one if the Old Man didn't learn to keep his head down soon.

John Murray well understood the Marine Corps concept of leading from the front. That was drilled into every Shavetail's head from the first day of Officer Candidate School. The Old Man took it to the extreme, though. He had shoved grunts out of the way at 0910 on August 7 when they first hit the beach on the Canal, trying to advance, advance, advance. It had all started off just right, so very easy, all according to the Pearl script. Then the Japanese got involved.

The first amphibious invasion by American forces in World War II, which actually encompassed assaults on three islands, caught the Japanese

The real delivery vehicles of the South Pacific: the native canoe. *Diane Bumba Collection.*

construction garrison completely off guard. The engineers of the emperor gave ground quickly, leaving the airfield on the Canal to the Americans within thirty-six hours. The Japanese did not fight wars with construction battalions, however. The First Marine Division was about to come face to face with the enemy on land, sea and air.

From the northeast came the Zeros, Bettys and Kates, the Japanese still holding air superiority throughout the Pacific. From bases to the north and northwest, Imperial Japanese Navy battleships and destroyers provided protection for the troop ships bringing reinforcements to the islands. The sixteen thousand Marines armed with bolt-action rifles and ten days of ammunition quickly found that easy landings had left them in a most precarious position—and then made especially precarious when twenty-four hours after the initial landings, the U.S. Navy was gone.

Proving that admirals protecting their fleets have more discretion than Marines seizing an island, the carrier task force assigned to the Guadalcanal withdrew from action the day after the landings, soon followed by the supply ships that had only been half unloaded. Eventually, they would return as American air power grew, but by that time, the Marines had time to experience snipers, banzai charges and infiltration as a daily occurrence. What the Japanese couldn't shoot at, dysentery had disabled—20 percent of the invaders down with the illness within two weeks of arrival. It would be three long months in hell and three major land battles for the 1st Division on the islands, and Chippewa Lake's John Murray saw it all.

He was there, right beside the Old Man when they stormed across what would be Henderson Field and cleared the Japanese from the tree line beyond. Murray was standing beside the Old Man when news came of Edson's stand up on the ridge when the Japanese counterattack came. Every day and every night, he stuck with the Old Man, even when the snipers had them zeroed in, the two Marines trusting in luck a lot more than common sense when it was them against the world. After three months, they made it; they'd come out the other side, and the Japanese were just about gone. The army would handle it after November, with Murray and the boys off to Australia to get ready for the next round. It was Christmas Down Under, the only regret being that the Old Man wouldn't be there. Pearl Harbor brass had other plans. They seemed to think he needed to meet the president.

The Old Man, Marine General Alexander Archie Vandergrift, recipient of the Congressional Medal of Honor for his bravery on Guadalcanal, whose adjutant through it all just happened to be Major John C. Murray, just another of the lost heroes from a place called little old Medina County, USA.

The Man Who Would Become Judge

January 10, 2013

It was a truism of 1942 Medina that wherever two or more gathered together, C.B. McClure was sure to be there. The grandson of a notoriously firm jurist, McClure had just begun his own law career as the war broke out. Given a sense of civic duty a little too often forgotten, the young attorney had better things to do than appear in court. He was out to win the war right here in Medina County.

There were air raid committees to join and rationing boards to sit on that first full year of conflict. C.B. McClure joined every organization and was a part of every bond drive the county had, trying to do more and more on every front back home knowing that there would be one more duty for the local boy making good. Having served his nation well at home, C.B. McClure set off to be a dogface, ground-pounding GI.

The details are sketchy, but somehow a socially active attorney from a small town became a socially active enlisted man as well. He could have been an officer, a licensed attorney always being needed in a bureaucracy, but C.B. McClure chose to work his way through the ranks from the bottom up, to find the way things really worked. By April 11, 1945, he'd made it to sergeant and managed to miss about every opportunity for combat. He made up for it one day in the field as their jeep rounded a bend and came to a stop. C.B. McClure came face to face with hell.

It was at Konzentrationslager Buchenwald, a work camp where more than fifty thousand died during World War II, that Sergeant McClure encountered evil as he wandered the grounds, surrounded by emaciated skeletons of the dead and what was left of the living. This had not been an extermination camp; it was slave labor, at least in theory. It was also a camp where human skin was used as decoration in the hobby shop. The Holocaust, Buchenwald and the hundreds of other camps just like it were the real reasons the Germans lost the war.

The Holocaust, as it is known now, was the German nation's attempt to exterminate the undesirable element, whatever that might have been, from the "master race." It is easy to stereotype and assume that the hideous crimes were exacted solely against the Jewish members of European society. In fact Gypsies, homosexuals, communists, Cossacks, trade unionists, educators, members of the clergy and even prisoners of war would find their way into the camps. The 6 million figure that is given for the number killed is probably conservative, as there may have been another 2 million by war's end. Those facts are undeniable, as is the fact that the German nation was killing some of its very best friends in those camps.

Inside the wire of the death and labor camps were thousands of German veterans of World War I and their families—German nationalists who just happened to be Jewish. There is absolutely no evidence to this day suggesting that without the programs that created the Holocaust, virtually every human being who ended up in a camp would have been employed in support of the German war effort—6 million more soldiers and laborers, a frightening prospect for those who engage in alternative history or chose to ignore the past. For one young Medina County attorney, there was no way he would ever ignore what he had seen.

C.B. McClure had been an eyewitness to lampshades made of human skin and shrunken heads made from Russian POWs. He saw Buchenwald inmates die from kindness—to overfeed a starving man was as deadly as a gas chamber itself. In one building, he thought he had discovered corpses, bunks filled with the dead, until one raised his hand and McClure realized that they were all alive, walking skeletons. He saw the depths of depravity that had been a government's policy and never forgot long after he came back home.

Mac, as his loving wife, Dorothy, always called him, returned to Medina and a good life. He practiced his law but only until he decided to run for mayor. After that it was to be Judge McClure, a wise jurist who tried every day to do the right thing for one simple reason. Once upon a time on an April day, he'd seen the wrong of absolute evil.

C.B. McClure, just another sergeant, just another eyewitness to the unimaginable, but there would be others. Others who took matters into their own hands.

THE TOUGH GUYS OF MEDINA

January 17, 2013

Vic McEnroe, Bob Shane, Blake Friedt and Willie Buerge didn't consider themselves bad guys or hoodlums of some sort. Not one of them talked like Cagney or Edward G. Robinson. None of them had ever been to a speakeasy, let alone shot one up. They were just four ordinary kids who came from a rural county in Ohio called Medina and happened to have picked up a label. They were just one small part of Roosevelt's SS.

At least that's what the Germans called them and every other member of the 30th Infantry Division as 1944 wound on during World War II. It was the enemy's highest compliment. The rugged 30th were professional soldiers, highly trained and even more disciplined to achieve the objective, whatever that objective might be. The men of the 30th took pride in the tribute, the best of the best in the American army, equal to best of Germany, but it was a reputation well earned.

The boys of the 30th had always preferred to called themselves the "Old Hickory" Division. They had a past that dated all the way back to Andrew Jackson's time and a dispute with some Seminoles over a swamp called Florida. In every war since then, they'd come to the front, primarily with boys of the South manning the ranks. By the time World War II was underway, they weren't so particular, now accepting Yankees into the fold just as long as they could fight. It didn't take long, and all of the 30th proved that this was exactly what they had come to do.

They came ashore at Omaha Beach on D-Day plus 4, moving on to lead the breakout at St. Lo. It was there where they met their nemesis for the first time, the German 1st SS. As the Axis forces were driven back, the new nickname was earned from the Germans' respect. The 30th was on the march, never holding a position when it could advance—across France and then as the first American unit into Belgium, the first into Holland. The men drove the enemy back as they captured Aachen, more than a match for the finest in black with silver piping every step of the way. Then it all went bad. War was no longer business. All of a sudden, it became very, very personal.

The date was December 17, 1944, the time about 1:30 p.m. The place the Baugnez Crossroads, although the nearby village called Malmedy would forever be its label. The engagement that would eventually be known as the Battle of the Bulge wasn't even thirty-six hours old when a unit of the 30th Division, Battery B, of the 285th Field Artillery Forward Observer Battalion, came face to face with the devil.

It was 2nd Platoon, 3rd Pioneer Company, the Penal Section of 3rd Pioneer and 7th Panzer Company of Joachim Peiper's Panzer SS spearhead. Over the next ninety minutes that day, they would turn the tide of first the battle and then the war totally against Germany by shooting prisoners of war taken at Baugnez Crossroads. Their second mistake was that fifty-five Americans escaped to tell the story of what had happened that day. What had become a retreat that bordered on a rout suddenly turned back like savage dogs out to avenge a cause. The boys of the 30th Infantry would never be called Roosevelt's SS again. They were out to be the SS Hunters instead.

Because of the weather in the Ardennes Forest that winter, the bodies of the victims from the German atrocity were not recovered until January 13, 1945. It was not until the last of the snow was cleared away by members of the 291st Combat Engineers manning mine detectors that the true horror of the war crimes became clear. Every soldier knew that something else was clear: justice had to be achieved.

The boys of the 30th knew that the 291st had assigned a tough little sergeant, their OSS operative, to track down the guilty, but they did their share too. There is no indication that any regimental commander of the 30th ever issued written orders, as others did, that there would be no SS trooper taken prisoner for the duration of the war. A well-trained unit doesn't need written orders to understand justice, and no one would ever equate them to scum again.

The tough guys, the best in every way a soldier could be, but sometimes they could be quite human as well, especially when it came to the birds of England.

ALL A MATTER OF ROMANCE

February 14, 2013

He was a most handsome fellow in spite of being a Yank. Rather a bit of lamb actually, the American sergeant who liked to stroll the public grounds in Manchester, England, that late summer of 1944. He seemed to like the zoo, the eateries and even the flower gardens—not that anyone was noticing. Certainly not Mrs. Toll's daughter, Margaret, of the Auxiliary Territorial Services. A proper English lady simply didn't do that, certainly not. Right then, a good-looking sergeant and one beautiful girl were traveling down the path to make history all over again.

It is another of the incongruities of war that in the midst of chaos, true love blossoms like English roses. It was true when Alexander's soldiers discovered the allure of the Greek girls, when Romans savored Goths who were still blondes and when Genghis Khan's army took the first Russian mail-order brides. Whenever armies invade, it has always been inevitable that marriage is soon to follow. Back in World War II, it was almost like the entire concept was part of the master plan.

At train stations all across the United States were found the United Service Organizations, the combination of the YMCA, the YWCA, the National Catholic Community, the National Jewish Welfare Board, Traveler's Aid and the Salvation Army that we came to call the USO. Begun at a place called the Terminal Tower by a kid named Firestone in early 1941, the USO sites were stopover points for the traveling serviceman or servicewoman, a chance to relax, meet people and then move on. There was more than one love affair created in those terminals, but nothing like what was to come once those Yanks hit overseas.

Even though there were Officers Clubs and Enlisted Clubs at every United States military post in the world, it was a night on the town doing some of the local bird watching that held promise. A young soldier boy didn't need to pub crawl in London, Manchester, Leeds or anywhere else to appreciate British beauty. It seemed like they were almost everywhere, each one more beautiful than the one before. As long as the commanding officer kept signing those forty-eight-hour passes, the Yanks were going to keep looking—every once in a while even chatting one of the locals up, just in the name of international goodwill. Never dreaming that some of those conversations were about to add to the American melting pot.

About 15,000 young ladies of Australian birth would find a new home during or immediately after World War II as wives of American servicemen. About 20,000 German girls would go and do likewise. In fact, virtually every foreign nation that was home to an American base during the conflict would contribute a wife to the landscape that is the United States, but none could compare to the English. More than 100,000 Brits were to be galvanized Yanks. A beautiful proposition, but for one couple, it was first a matter of culture shock.

For one young sergeant, it was fine to be in the land of the Bentley, the Rolls-Royce and the MG TA, but they still drove on the wrong side of the road all the same. They had a monarchy with dukes, duchesses, earls, dames and who knows what, but a crown had something to do with a tuppence, whatever that was. Then there was the matter of the whole nation not even speaking English, even this little cutie who had caught his eye by the flower garden. A crescent wrench was a "spanner," a flashlight was a "torch," chips were "thins" and fries were "chips." A man couldn't hope to figure it out any more than a young English girl could figure out the United States.

The Great Excited States, where they were all either cowboys or lived in a skyscraper, was Mrs. Toll's daughter's concept of America. Always in a hurry, always talking too much, always too sure of themselves—no lady in her right mind would consider such a man, no matter how good looking or how nice he just happened to be. Even if he was a most noble lad indeed. No future at all.

Perhaps that's why three months after the day they met, they married and lived happily ever after, and seventy years later, she's still as beautiful as her British accent, living among those skyscrapers and cattle ranches of the Great Excited little old Medina County, USA.

THE PLACE CALLED SURIBACHI

February 21, 2013

They sell sports cards today just off the Square at 110 West Washington. Good people working hard to get by, and I do wish them well. I never had much interest in the subject they market, not able to hit a curveball and the Canadiens never really being interested in a five-foot, four-inch checking forward rather limiting my interest in sports today. I always look when I go by, though, every time, trying to hold on to one moment in the past. That afternoon a long time ago, I got to spend time with the legend.

His name was Lou Lowery, but I called him "Sir." He was quick to remind me that he worked for a living running Lou's Camera Shop—that title was reserved for officers. The habits of an aging Leatherneck sergeant never died, even though his fame almost has. For a few beautiful hours, I had the pleasure to sit and talk with the great man, although we really had little to say. It was more me just sitting there staring at the picture and

A photo that means little—a sailor capturing Marines getting into landing craft—except one-fourth of the men pictured will not be alive in twelve hours. Such was the cost of a place called Iwo Jima. *Diane Bumba Collection.*

then the man—the Marine Corps photographer for *Leatherneck* magazine who really was the first on top of Suribachi.

Just 556 feet above sea level, overlooking the hell that was Iwo Jima, Sergeant Lowery was on assignment to photograph the flag-raising over the island. He watched and waited as 3rd Platoon, E Company, 28th Marines' Charlie Lindberg, Harry Schrier, Hank Hansen and Ernie Thomas made their way to the summit with a set of colors from the transport *Missoula*, with Japanese fire still hot and heavy. It was all for morale, as capturing the island was still a month away, but nobody knew it right then. Nobody dreamed what was about to happen in another hour that made another man famous and Lou Lowery a footnote to history.

Down below on the beachhead, the brass couldn't see the flag that had gone up, at least as well as they wanted. The troops needed inspiration, a symbol that this battle had turned the American way. A bigger flag from an LST was secured and sent up to the top along with a photographer named Rosenthal. What would happen next will live forever.

Another look at the hell of Iwo Jima on February 19, 1945, when Rosenthal became immortal and Medina's Lou Lowery became a footnote. *National Archives and Records Administration, Dreyfuss Collection, 127.N-110249.*

It wasn't that Harlon Block, Frank Sousley, Jon Bradley, Mike Strank, Ira Hayes or Rene Gagnon were on top of that mountain waiting to raise flags or be heroes. They just happened to be there in one shell hole or another, trying to take out the enemy. Somebody yelled for some help. The Marines and their navy corpsman buddy found a pole, tied off the flag and put it up. It just happened that Joe Rosenthal of the Associated Press snapped a shot of it, one of hundreds he had and would take. The photograph that would be set into sculpture that is today the Marine Corps Memorial in Washington, D.C.

The future was not always kind to the men of Suribachi, even as the battle that was only supposed to take a few days ground on to an American victory. The island airfield would be captured, with the B-29s soon to find a temporary home there on their missions over Japan, but Frank Sousley, Harlon Block and Mike Strank never made it back. In fact, of the 250 men in their company, only 27 would survive without being a casualty at Iwo. The three flag raisers who did survive eventually wondered if their comrades hadn't been the lucky ones.

Gagnon, Hayes and Bradley survived the island to return to the United States as the heroes they never wanted to be. They were two Marines PFCs and a Pharmacist's Mate Second Class who happened to be in battle when fame came calling. They returned to the States for the Seventh War Bond Drive, more embarrassed by the adulation than flag-wavers. For Hayes in particular, it would be a rapid descent into his own hell of drunkenness, dying in an alcohol stupor before he was thirty-three. Of them all, only Joe Rosenthal would hold on to the fame he had never really searched for.

To him, it was one of hundreds of photos, but the Pulitzer committee saw it differently that year. So did a nation. Rosenthal's career was set, his work now forever considered art. He would travel the world in prominence, sincerely modest as he downplayed his effort. It was just another photo, taken sixty-eight years ago Saturday, and a guy named Lou faded away in a camera shop in little old Medina County, USA.

THE QUEEN OF THE SEAS

February 28, 2013

It was a ship of many lives, this keel laid down on March 9, 1943, that would first become the SS *Stanford White*. Named for a prominent architect of the time, the *White* would take just thirty-nine days from start to finish for construction. From the dockyards of California Shipbuilding of Los Angeles, it set sail south and then east through the Panama Canal to that most unenviable and yet so essential career as a Liberty ship.

They were the workhorses of World War II, oceangoing cargo ships manned by the truly forgotten veterans, the Merchant Marine sailors. By the thousands, Liberty ships hauled the essentials from the States to England, France, Africa, Russia and everywhere else there was an Allied port. For the majority, it was a career of endless back and forth, dodging the remnants of the U-boats in the Atlantic, left to be a seldom-mentioned note of history. For the SS *Stanford White*, it was once over, once back and then a higher calling.

It was at the end of September in 1943 that Hull No. 738, the SS *Stanford White*, set sail out of New York on its only Liberty duty. It joined a convoy at sea, carrying supplies for the ever-increasing American forces in England in preparation for the invasion. Docking at Liverpool the second week of October, the *White* was unloaded and back in a returning convoy 120 hours later. It docked at New York after a totally uneventful mission, the cargo career over. Transferred to the U.S. Army command, a new ship was born.

More than nine hundred tons were added to the reconfigured four-hundred-plus-foot hull. Gone were the weapons to guard against submarine attack, as was the empty cargo space below decks. What had been the SS *Stanford White* was remade into a floating hospital, initially named the *Poppy* per government policy. In a matter of days, though, it would be rechristened to a more appropriate name. In August 1944, the Hospital Ship *Blanche F. Sigman*, named to honor one killed on the Anzio beachhead, set sail in the cause of the wounded.

Lieutenant Sigman had been a surgical nurse who came ashore within a few hours of the American landing at Anzio in Operation Shingle. It was an end run around the Germans holding the Gustav Line near Monte Cassino, part of General Mark Clark's plan to take Rome before its destruction. For Blanche Sigman, strategy didn't matter—only the worst cases of wounded as they were carried in from the attack. On the sandy shore, she worked inside the regimental aid station until the morning of February 7, 1944, when a German bomb killed the dying and those who tried to save them. The ship that bore her name set sail in August 1944 to carry on one brave nurse's work.

With an urgent sense of duty, the *Sigman* left Charleston, South Carolina, for England, its first mission to return troopers gravely wounded at D-Day

Europe to the States for advanced treatment. The ship received its human cargo at Liverpool and immediately set sail back to the Carolinas. It truly was a hospital as well as a ship, with surgeries taking place more often than inspections. It was just the beginning of a glorious career.

After arriving in Charleston again and resupplying, the *Sigman* moved on to what were missions of ironic compassion, the ship being sent to the Mediterranean, evacuating some of the very same troopers who had stood on the beachhead when Lieutenant Sigman was killed, now wounded themselves. Throughout the war it sailed, seeing ports like Oran, Gibraltar and Naples. As the war came to a conclusion in Europe, its final duties were to transport the nurses and Red Cross workers back home. As 1947 came to a close, its duty done, all that was left to the queen of the seas were two final injustices.

America didn't need Liberty ships once we stopped fighting wars and went to police actions. The Hospital Ship *Blanche F. Sigman* was decommissioned in 1948, mothballed on the James River in Virginia for years until finally scrapped for $145,115 in 1974, just another forgotten ship that did its duty. Just like its namesake, Lieutenant Blanche F. Sigman, just another nurse no one ever heard of.

Blanche F. Sigman, war casualty, war hero, who gave up her life a long way from her home in Medina County, Ohio.

A LONG WAY FROM A HARDWARE STORE

March 21, 2013

If you didn't know Steve Stephenson, you aren't Old Medina. For nearly eight decades, he reigned supreme as the king of nuts, bolts and washerless faucets from his throne inside Medina Hardware on South Court. Surrounded by millions of pieces that might one day be needed by somebody, Mr. Stephenson was absolutely the definitive source of home improvement information in the county. It's unfortunate that most of the same county never knew what the great man did during World War II. Just a simple duty. He was the one who made sense out of the greatest mess in the South Pacific.

It was mid-August 1942 when word reached the tall young man that he had been commissioned as a second lieutenant in the Engineers Amphibian Command because of his wealth of experience. The military seemed to

Above: A welcoming committee somewhere in the South Pacific, dressed in their best. *Diane Bumba collection.*

Left: The universal currency of war throughout the world: American cigarettes. *Diane Bumba Collection.*

think that it had found the perfect candidate to correct everything that had gone wrong for its Marines two weeks before at a place called Guadalcanal. For all the planning, for all the military brainpower, the American armed forces quickly realized with the first invasion of a Japanese-held island that we had absolutely no idea of what we were doing.

The United States Navy was magnificent from the very beginning of the war until its conclusion at moving troops from a point of embarkation to a location off shore of wherever the action was supposed to be. The Marines and the army were superb themselves once they were ashore. It was that gap between where the ship anchored and the beach that was the mysterious element of the equation, the two thousand yards or so of open space when soldiers, sailors and Marines were the most vulnerable. Unfortunately for thousands of those servicemen, the solution the military came up with bordered on outright murderous.

They are the images we associate with the invasion at Normandy now, the Landing Ship Tank (LST) and the Landing Craft Personnel (LCP). Plywood in construction, they were more like floating coffins than sailing craft. Coxswains, the captains of these small vessels, stood in plain sight in order to steer and in plain target to a waiting enemy. The crafts, should they reach the beach despite being slow and tempting targets on the sail to shore, dropped their doors, and troopers aboard funneled out into battle, more often than not met by waiting concentrated machine gun fire. The LST and LCP did have one consolation though. At least they weren't amtracks.

Not the terrible excuse of passenger rail service inflicted on America today, amtracks of World War II were the all-terrain vehicle of the South Pacific. Resembling a tank without a turret, these vehicles were supposed to traverse sea and shore by propeller and then tracks, passing over reef and sand with ease to deliver a squad to battle. Delivery was one thing, but the first generation of amtracks had no exit doors. What came next often times ended with eighteen more Marine casualties, jumping over the sides into battle and dead before they were able to stand. It was into this confusion that Second Lieutenant Willard A. Steve Stephenson was sent to make it all right.

Slowly but surely for the duration of the war, the lieutenant and those around him worked out the details of turning bad designs and worse planning into something other than death traps. The war in the Pacific was an aberration; at no time before or since in the history of man had so many invasions been attempted. There were no textbooks and no standard operating procedure—just wise, thoughtful men like Steve Stephenson

Contrary to the Hollywood image, the locals of the Pacific were not some of the "Beautiful People." *Diane Bumba Collection.*

doing the best they could. Planning, improving and perfecting until the very last day of the war—glad that one last plan, the landing on the home islands of Japan, never had to be attempted.

Lieutenant Stephenson came home to become a local legend and a generous philanthropist, his beneficences to this day helping many. The store was his real home, and hardware was what he really knew, much more so than landing craft. Despite what the army had told him about being an expert, Steve Stephenson never believed that he knew any more about that subject than the law allowed. In fact, he always wondered how he'd ever gotten the job, but it was the army after all.

Steve Stephenson's sole qualification to be the landing craft expert was that he'd once been the commodore of the Chippewa Lake Yacht Club, 380 acres of ocean in the middle of Medina County, Ohio.

REAL NAMES A SOLDIER EARNS

March 28, 2013

They call it "respecting the individual," the corporate policy of one of Medina's big-box stores that ensures equality among the staff. In theory, as long as all employees call one another by their first names, it is a workplace of happiness and harmony. No titles, no ranks, just first names and no more. With no Mr. Jones, no Assistant Manager David and certainly no nicknames like "Weedhopper" or "Crypt-Keeper," the store operates as a jovial retailer where this policy does establish one thing for sure: whoever came up with the idea that this is a definition of respect never served in the military.

Long before Galius the Gaul and Visogoth Vicius marched with Caesar's legions, soldiers had saddled one another with nicknames. These labels were, in fact, the greatest form of appreciation in ancient times—a mark of acceptance as being a brother in arms. In armies that could well be away from home for entire generations, the military became true brothers, the only family many would ever know. It can't be any surprise, therefore, that as the troops began to mobilize after Pearl Harbor, the tradition of the nickname as earned respect was about to become a required part of military life again, whether some of Medina County cared to admit it or not.

To understand the art form that is a military-issue nickname, certain protocols, procedures and minimum standards must be understood. A

RECREATION BUILDING
NO. 211

CANTEEN OPEN
1130 1930

A recruit class at Great Lakes that defied all odds. They all would make it home one day. *Diane Bumba Collection.*

nickname can never, under any circumstances, be chosen by the recipient. It must be bestowed, granted as if a royal crown, worn proudly for the duration. Nicknames cannot be traded nor may they be duplicated within a unit. They are as individual as a fingerprint and are, each and every time, well earned over a course of events. How those names are determined is a doctoral dissertation waiting to be written.

Of all military nicknames, none is more common nor more obvious than the one assigned to a former resident of the Lone Star State, "Tex." No other geographic entity can compare. Ohio does well with a derivative of Buckeye, "Buck," but most of the other forty-eight aren't often considered. Jersey perhaps, Rhode Island never, California a rarity and Oregon ridiculous. Having assigned Tex to a local born in Austin and Buck to a Medina County native once of Ohio State and by 1942 in olive drab, the remaining ten names in an all-star Medina twelve-man squad would then require an appraisal of personal appearance, habit or peculiarity to form that perfect unit.

In terms of height, only those blessed and fortunate enough to be less than five feet, six inches would earn the moniker "Shorty," but only after it was offered in a non-derogatory manner. To belittle a tent mate for the sole reason of feeling better about one's self would run the risk of being branded

One squared-away sailor, Robert Cotton. *Diane Bumba Collection.*

as "Toothy" or "Toothless" as a result. At the same time, a towering giant of six feet, four inches and nearly 250 pounds was the ideal "Tiny," even the military appreciating the understatement from time to time. Having fulfilled four of the virtually mandatory slots in the squad nickname roster, it would then simply be a matter of waiting and watching human nature to assign the rest.

Despite a soldier's right to complain about the mess hall, it is inevitable that at least one squad member actually enjoyed army food and therefore was designated "Chow Hound." "Lefty" was one of seven fortunate enough to be a southpaw, while "Swede" earned his label for being blonde and blue-eyed even though he never had been outside Brunswick before 1942. "Cow Pie" once slept in the wrong place in a French farmer's field, "Romeo" made eyes at the same farmer's daughter and "Bloodhound" could pick up a German's trail at two hundred yards. "Chief" looked very Indian for an Italian, and "Bull" had that kind of strength, and that courage, to make it home. They all made it home, back to Medina, leaving a war, and all those nicknames, far behind. What they left for us must never be forgotten.

Corporate America of today never will understand the concept of brotherhood forged in a fire that we know as World War II. A brotherhood that destroyed an evil and then reformed a nation, not for obscene profit but for common good. Twelve colorful guys, just part of the equation, part of the brotherhood of military men that spanned the globe—all the way to Alaska once.

A DEADLIEST CATCH OF A MEDAL

April 11, 2013

It's the greatest male soap opera in the history of television. April has returned, and with it comes the Discovery Channel's addictive series *Deadliest Catch*. It's time for households far removed from the Bering Sea to board the *Time Bandit* with Andy and the *Northwestern* with Sig to set sail. It's time to spend an hour each week breaking in the greenhorns and watch eagles soar somewhere other than Chippewa Lake, to wage war against the elusive king crab in an ocean battleground—one battleground that Medina's Vance Grimes knew all too well.

Seventy years ago today, Seaman Second Class Grimes and the rest of the crew set sail out of Dutch Harbor, Alaska Territory. There were no crab pots on the deck, just stacks of ammunition ready to be loaded. The objective was not million-dollar hauls to support America's Chinese buffets but something a little more vital to the national effort called World War II. The mission that day and for days to come was to eliminate about three thousand troopers of the Imperial Japanese Army, troopers who were just around the corner five hundred miles away.

The northernmost front of the American side of World War II is often forgotten as well as misunderstood. The Pacific Theater dealt with incredible expanses of space for the most part, thousands of miles of water to be crossed to repress the Rising Sun. At the same time, it is only ninety miles from the outer Aleutian Islands to America's uneasy ally in the European war, the Russians, who throughout most of the conflict wanted nothing to do with a second front against the Oriental. Knowing that, the Japanese moved to take advantage of the situation by creating one of the most bizarre outposts in the history of warfare.

Beginning as a diversion disguising true Japanese intentions to Midway the year before, the invasion of Alaska had no intention other than to be a thorn in American long-range plans. The Imperial Staff was primarily concerned with the potential use of the islands as bomber bases for an assault on Tokyo and other targets. After an obligatory bombing of the American installation at Dutch Harbor, totally oblivious to the natural resources of the Alaskan Territory as well as American weaknesses, the Japanese withdrew to Kiska Island in the Aleutians to establish a defensive base. They quickly learned a basic fact of life by the Bering Sea: if nobody else lives there, don't you live there either.

For just over a year, the Japanese invasion garrison survived life on an island devoid of fresh water, human or animal habitation and virtually all vegetation. Coupled with those issues went the natural elements we watch each week on *Deadliest Catch*: hurricanes, temperatures that can reach fifty below zero and winds that have no beginning and no end. Supplies were only available from their own ships running the submarine gauntlet across the northern Pacific, the effect on American plans negligible. Even the Shinto religion has a hell, and it was called Kiska then, but it was a hell that the United States military had to eliminate.

So it was that in April 1943, navy ships made steam out of Dutch and bound for glory. For Seaman Second Class Grimes of Medina, it quickly became a matter of survival, with Japanese destroyers off shore supporting supply ships and catching the Americans off guard on their first sortie. By any definition, it was an Imperial victory, the Stars and Stripes quickly driven back, casualties many on the decks and below—casualties that included a seaman second class.

Barely clinging to life, Vance Grimes was evacuated from the combat zone stateside as the next assault on Kiska was planned. He was still in a West Coast hospital improving slowly by that second week in August when the American assault forces left Dutch Harbor to avenge a defeat. The naval force would end up missing the battle completely.

On the morning of August 15, 1943, covered by a thick fog, the entire enemy garrison on Kiska was evacuated by their own ships in just one hour and escaped back to Japan without a single casualty. Just about the moment the fog lifted and the Americans, who had been less than a mile away, came ashore with guns blazing at a deserted island, they were pinning a Purple Heart on Seaman Second Class Grimes.

Just another good sailor, wounded in battle for the island nobody wanted, miles away from a former neighbor who spent the war working for something almost nobody knew anything about.

NOBODY TOLD HIM ANYTHING

April 25, 2013

Willard DeWitt loved his cottage out at Chippewa Lake. Any chance he got to spend a weekend there was time well spent. There was just one place he'd rather be than Shady Slope Lane during those summer months of World War II. Like almost everybody else, he would have given up almost anything to get into the service and be in that war. Unlike everybody else, he knew that he'd never get into uniform. He was what they called an Essential Civilian Employee.

So great was the answer to Uncle Sam's call when war broke out that it became necessary to mandate that certain positions in the civilian job market not be permitted to join the military. As much as the army and navy needed men and women, certain industries needed experts to keep things running at home to produce that which the government needed even more. It was the trap that electrical engineer Willie DeWitt fell into, but he really didn't know why at first. The answer to that would be one of the great secrets of World War II.

He'd always seen himself as more of the Errol Flynn kind of guy, the last of the great swashbucklers—so much so that he'd taken up the saber and founded the Ohio State Fencing Club when he was in college. It was only natural that a dashing daredevil like himself would head up the next Dawn Patrol, complete with leather jacket and silk scarf. He knew how to fly—that was another college adventure—and he certainly was willing to be the next air ace, but Uncle Sam turned down that request in 1942. What the government didn't know was that Willie DeWitt was far from finished trying to do his part.

If not piloting a B-17 over Berlin, DeWitt was more than willing to take an assignment as one of the madmen of the military, the combat photographer. He knew the world of F-stops and darkrooms as well as he knew the controls of a Piper. Eventually, he would open DeWitt's Photo Supply in Rocky River and make a success out of it, but not in 1943. Uncle Sam insisted that he was much more valuable where he was, not snapping shots for *Leatherneck* magazine or *Stars and Stripes*. With that official government refusal, Willard DeWitt had almost had enough. If the military wouldn't let him in, there must be somebody who could explain what on earth was so essential about being a simple electrical engineer.

After all, he was just another guy working at the Cleveland Illuminating Company. He'd get up in the morning, drive to work, put in a six-day

Essential workers. For all they might have wanted to go to war as soldiers and sailors, their duties at home were far too valuable, their work too secret, for the effort at hand. *Sharon Beachy Collection.*

workweek and make sure that the grid kept running. Sure, sure, there was a little excitement when a summer thunderstorm took out the power at the airport for a while, but it was nothing out of the ordinary, at least for Cleveland. No reason for some one-star brass hat to get excited. Willie had it covered, nothing to it. A chimp could do the job. Or a general. That really made DeWitt's buddy Bill laugh.

Bill had been a fraternity brother of Willie's at Ohio State, a fellow engineer with a little more interest in the mechanical instead of electrical. He had a good job someplace—Willie wasn't real sure where, but Bill always stopped by whenever business brought him to Cleveland. In fact, Bill even stayed at the house when he was in town. That summer of 1944, when the power went out and Willie expressed his opinion on military commanders, it was Bill who finally let the cat out of the bag as to exactly what "essential" meant.

It was a Sunday morning when they pulled up to the building that is today the I-X Center in Cleveland. Willie knew of it; it was on the grid he was in charge of, but it was just another building, another place that needed power, another place his buddy Bill called home. Bill was the chief design engineer on the top-secret B-29 Superfortress being constructed in Cleveland, a fact that he'd neglected to tell Willie or anybody else.

Willie DeWitt was at his cottage in Chippewa Lake when the first atomic bomb dropped in 1945. The neighbors celebrated. A war was coming to an end, but he just grinned. That was his power that put that plane in the air that dropped the bomb that made it end. Being essential had its benefits after all. It was just too bad that DeWitt was never quite as essential as one most endearing sergeant.

A Mother Hen of the Military

May 16, 2013

Nobody could have accused Seville's Clarence Gilbert of being a character in one of Bill Maudlin's cartoons in *Stars and Stripes*. There was no Joe or Willie in that squared-away trooper. The tie was on, the leggings were in place and the boots were shined seven days a week for Gilbert. There was no time for the trooper to be Sad Sack anyway, not when he had to be Mother Hen all the time. Any doubt about that fact, and one just had to ask General Bradley.

General Omar N. Bradley, West Point '15, classmate to Eisenhower and the only man who could control Patton—that General Bradley. The GI's general, who began World War II as a simple divisional commander and ended up commanding armies in the field and in the occupation of Germany. A busy man with much on his mind, Bradley had an ace in the hole to keep his life in order all throughout the war: a skinny aide by the name of Clarence Gilbert.

To be a general's aide during World War II was roughly equivalent to being butler to an English lord in the most refined of country estates. The aide laid out the general's uniform only after he'd ensured that it was clean and free of rip or tear. The boss's shirt was pressed, his tie cleaned, the slacks creased and both helmet and shoes polished to perfection, all before waking the great man up to start another day. Then came the small matters of making sure that his food was right and coffee hot, the day's schedule in order and that there was absolutely nothing in the way of surprises ahead. Then they could get to work.

Throughout the day, the aide was at the general's side wherever he went and in whatever he was doing, catering to every need whether real or imagined. Then, as evening came, it was time to answer all the correspondence, write the endearing letter home to the family and then make sure that the general got to bed at a reasonable hour in a most reasonable condition. It was duty that Mother Hen Gilbert loved every second of, every day of every week, watching history as it happened.

Throughout the Italian invasion, on to the breakout at Normandy and into the Bulge, Clarence Gilbert was there beside Omar Bradley every step of the way. He lit Eisenhower's cigarette and heard Patton's tirades while serving his general. As the war wound down, the general rewarded his caregiver with the Bronze Star, a coveted decoration for a job well done. Having already seen so much, Clarence Gilbert got to see the final act as well.

Remembering all those reports and letters that Gilbert had typed so neatly, General Bradley appointed the Seville lad to the court reporter's pool for the Nuremberg trials of Nazi war criminals. Day after day, he stared at evil, taking down every word they uttered in the defenses for their crimes that had no explanation. Clarence Gilbert was there as Goering was led to the dock. He watched and listened as the madman Hess attempted to justify his deeds. At every trial, he took notes, attempting to stay neutral, the simple court reporter watching history unfold, knowing all along how many would end up.

Clarence Gilbert understood that much each day as the court recessed and he'd take a break outside. It was there he made conversation with one sergeant who'd been with the 291st Combat Engineers during the war and now the construction foreman for the army hangman. That was a tough job, enough to make a man crazy or at least sleep with the lights on for ten years to come, enough to convince Clarence Gilbert that he'd had his fill of this life in the military and needed to get back to where he could be a real mother hen. Back in a place called East Liverpool, Ohio.

That's where the real ace of General Omar Bradley's staff headed when the discharge came through, on to a life where his talents could really be appreciated, living with his mother. There he could take care of people who mattered just as much as some silly old general. His days with those beasts in uniform were over; for the rest of his life, it would be all about his girls.

The general's best aide became East Liverpool's finest beautician. Another one of the eyewitnesses to history, another of the great characters of life, Clarence Gilbert, a character almost as large as a man called Jack.

About the Last Hero on Earth

June 6, 2013

His classmates called him Puss, but for Medina High School's Jack Ryan, it was never very clear how he ever earned that moniker back in the early 1940s. Not that he ever had the time to worry about it, not with the schedule he was on. After all, somewhere, sometime, there had to a party going on some place, and he had to make an entrance.

Whether it was at the stamp club, the historical society, a meeting of library officials or just a walk uptown, every outing was a personal appearance for Ryan. The hair was meticulous, the slacks creased and the shirt was ironed before the great man would grace the public with his presence. It was almost a dandified presentation, but it was all a matter of a most exacting past.

Between the time Ryan left Medina in 1943 and his return thirty some years later, most of his career was one that spanned the globe in the United States diplomatic corps. Far from the movie version of spies and secret agents, this was a life where protocol and place settings mattered more than whoever coaches the Browns this year. Holding a wine glass by the stem and not the goblet or the proper technique in heating a brandy did far more for international goodwill than any summit conference. It was a world of poses and postures that fit Ryan like a glove, even if he was a man of a couple of secrets.

Her name was Grace, and she was the absolute love of Jack's life. They met in federal service and took assignments only when they could be together. Hopelessly devoted to each other, they knew from almost day one that their future had to be together, even after retirement called. The only problem was that Jack's mother did not approve.

It was another time that today's generation often cannot understand, where religious persuasions dictated personal relationships. Mother did not approve of Grace's interpretation of Christianity. As long as she lived, her boy Jack would never marry someone like that. Jack Ryan was a man of those traditional values, honoring his father and mother to say the least, and he respected his mother's wishes. He never did marry Gracie. He just spent his entire life beside her.

Every day, Gracie would step out of her apartment, dressed to the nines and step next door to have breakfast with Jack and Mother. A leisurely stroll up through town, playing the social gadflies, generally led to lunch on the square. From there it was back home, for Mother's nap and an afternoon of cards before the old lady got her dinner and went to bed. Then it became time for Jack and Gracie to go out and hold court somewhere.

Even when Ohio winters were becoming too much and Jack wanted a Florida getaway, it was Grace who bought the place next to his. Mother always thought that Grace was a very nice person and that it was good her son had a friend, but it never was anything more than that. That's what Mrs. Ryan always said, whether she believed it or not. Finally passing in her late nineties, Mother always knew it that way. After all those years, free at last, Jack and Grace still never did marry. They just stayed in love, holding on to that one other secret Jack held so well: he had once been a film star.

Once in a while, you can still see the great man on celluloid today, although you have to be a cable channel subscriber. A carrier that has things like the Military Channel or the History networks. He was younger, and he wasn't wearing the glasses we all remember him for, but it is Jack Ryan all the same. The retired expert of diplomatically protocol who wouldn't get a fingernail dirty seems to have known how to operate heavy equipment.

Sixty-nine years ago today, at the Normandy beachhead. The Germans on the bluffs to one side and the invasion ships at sea to the other. American troopers are in the middle, trying to scale the cliffs. The invasion was only a couple of hours old, and there came a solitary bulldozer clearing the way to bring up more supplies, old Puss at the wheel. A small detail the great man always left out in the course of casual conversation.

American diplomat, American war hero, just another of the multitude of modest characters that were the Greatest. A war hero when sometimes heroes have yet to be recognized for how great they really were.

THE JACK OF THE DUST

June 13, 2013

The hoisting of an anchor was a blessing to those few silent ones aboard every vessel of the United States Navy in World War II. A ship at sea let the invisibles have an extra half an hour in the rack, trying to find sleep. They could rest all the way to 0430 while underway. Not at all like in port, when the boatswain's pipe sounded at 0400 each and every day. A half an hour's extra sleep was about the only blessing there ever was for the sailors the navy called the Jacks of the Dust.

For fifteen hours a day, seven days a week, they labored at their assignment. Never seen, never heard, and most were never even known by name by crewmen outside their work area. With any luck, there might be an hour topside, the only daylight they would see was the last hour of twilight during summer months. For the rest of the day, it was down below, laboring away and privy to every single secret there was on ship.

The Jack of the Dust was there when the captain opened his sailing orders, but nobody saw him. He was there when one of the radio officers admitted that the dice were crooked in last night's game, but the guilty had no clue they were overheard. When the top-secret operational orders were opened while at sea, it was the Jack of the Dust reading them along with the skipper, long before the navigator knew to set a new course. It was a world of confidentiality that Medina's Jimmy Johnson knew so very well.

Being the silent man of an oceangoing ship wasn't exactly what the hero of the gridiron had in mind when he enlisted. He and Bobby Hodnet saw themselves as more of the gunnery kind of guys when they joined up in June 1943. In a perfect world, they both would have been shipped to Norfolk, to get into navy shape under the watchful eye of an instructor there named Woody Hayes. The navy wasn't perfect in 1943, and the two locals found themselves at Great Lakes.

For eight long weeks, they learned to be navy recruits, right out of the 1940 edition of the *Bluejacket Manual*. They drilled, they learned to stow their gear and they learned to read signals and fire weapons. No different than anyone else. They graduated from camp and were sailors. Sailors who must by navy regulation be Jacks of the Dust.

In silence they served, good sailors doing their job, privy to secrets and working long, hard hours. Hoping for an hour topside when at sea, just to know that there was life beyond their duty station. That there was more to navy life than washing the captain's china and clearing the plates after supper. An official navy title that dated back to the eighteenth century, Jack of the Dust, that we now call a busser. The only entry-level seagoing position that the navy thought thousands of men capable of doing simply because they were black.

Even though the United States Navy had been the first fully integrated branch of service during the Civil War, the reality of a man's ability was long forgotten by 1941. It was segregation at its worse, and yet thousands of true American patriots of African heritage like Johnson and Hodnut stepped forward year after year. The captain might never know Jimmy's name, but it didn't matter. It was all about serving the nation, however that service was defined.

Jimmy Johnson would only be mentioned twice in the *Medina County Gazette* during the war years. Both times it wasn't about his duty; it was the color of his skin, black servicemen being a novelty. There were no medals or unit citations, just another sailor doing what he was assigned somewhere in the South Pacific in what would be total war. Knowing all throughout the day and night that deckhands sank just like Jacks of the Dust, he hoped he'd get home and get on with some living.

No. 64 did make it back, forty years the GM employee, sixty-five years the devoted husband and seventy years the true gentleman. We remember him for the quick feet and sharp moves of a great halfback, but that was just a small part of the real man who served and survived a world we really can't comprehend.

Jimmy Johnson, No. 64 who was No. 1, another of the Greatest of little old Medina County, USA.

An American Reason for War

June 27, 2013

It is a truism of all things military that the English fight for the Crown, the French fight for the Republic and Americans fight for souvenirs. Ever since the first British cannonball rolled to a stop at Breed's Hill near Boston, American servicemen have always seen the merit in finding something on a battlefield worth keeping. In World War II, scavenging was just about an art form, one that an entire nation would soon embrace.

For the average GI, there was one Holy Grail of souvenir in each theater of operation. For those in Europe, it was a German officer's Luger pistol; in the Pacific, it was a Japanese sword. A trooper who acquired either could fairly well write his own ticket in terms of trade bait with his tent mates or behind the lines at Supply. They were the grand prizes of memorabilia but far from the only coveted items for the good American soldier.

There was always a market for Swiss wristwatches, daggers and Iron Crosses taken off Germans who no longer had any need of the equipment all throughout the war in Europe. In Asia, the market was a little tighter, fairly well limited to Japanese medals being good and headbands even better to swap out for an extra case of beer. Thriving business, just as long as a soldier never got caught.

Even then, amateur photographers had trouble getting light settings just right.
Diane Bumba Collection.

Not so much by military authority, even though there are articles of war against looting, but by the enemy—the possession of contraband was an issue. The Japanese in general, and the German's SS in particular, took dim views of their former comrades' personal possessions in the hands of Americans. It was generally a death sentence, but to the GIs, it was almost worth the risk. After all, it was all for the folks back home.

While military hardware was usually stowed in footlockers and duffel bags for that glorious day when a trooper shipped home, hundreds of enemy flags, armbands and uniform patches did make their way stateside via the U.S. Mail throughout the war. They were trophies of war, two generations from understanding collectors' markets and obscene prices. Mementos fairly won, proudly sent home and even more proudly displayed in homes and businesses all around the country. So great was the American obsession for souvenirs in World War II that even the government itself got involved. Once upon a time, it brought Wadsworth an enemy submarine.

It will be seventy years ago next week, just in time for the local Fourth of July parade, that the *HA-19* arrived. This was America's first trophy of World War II, one of the Japanese midget subs that had attempted to attack Pearl

Harbor. Eighty feet long, six feet wide and ten feet in height, the emperor's weapon of death had even more meaning to a town that had lost one of its own in the sneak attack. It was a matter of pride, a victory over Japan, even if nobody in Wadsworth realized the true reason for the sub's capture. Far from demonstrating military prowess by the U.S. Navy, the *HA-19* had become American property only because it had been manned by two of the most incompetent sailors in the history of the sea.

Their names were Kazuo Sakamaki and Kiyoshi Inagaki, the Jonas Gumby and Bob Gilligan of the Imperial Japanese Navy. At 3:30 a.m. on December 7, 1941, they left the submarine *I-24* inside their midget sub and made their way to Pearl Harbor fifty miles away. The mission was to launch two torpedoes as a part of the attack on the American base, at least in theory. In actuality, it was an exercise in finding new and inventive ways to foul things up.

From the time they left the mother ship until nine o'clock that evening, the Japanese salts managed to find Pearl Harbor by accident because of a broken compass, ram the same reef five times trying to get into the harbor, pass out twice from battery fumes while trying to fire their torpedoes and then run aground the first time they were attacked. One would drown, the other became POW no. 1 in America, but we had a trophy, a souvenir to celebrate one Fourth of July.

To the people of Wadsworth, it didn't matter how it was captured. It was a victory all the same, and they lined up to cheer America that day. The first victory of the war that redefined one way or another the world, at least in terms of temporal issues. When it came to the heavenly—and the hell because of it—that was a matter for a man named Ward.

A Man of God in Time of War

July 4, 2013

It's Independence Day, another of the multitude of holidays in the United States that have long since lost their true meaning. Let's be honest. This most sacred day of the American form of government is now defined by the parade at Chippewa Lake, a cookout in the backyard and then fireworks someplace. None of it seems to have a whole lot to do with the founding of an experimental form of self-rule, let alone freedom. Perhaps it's because most of us never had to deal with the alternative. We might never truly understand, but then again, we weren't Ralph Ward.

It's been three full generations since the great man decided to follow the great commission, but that had nothing to do with captain's bars or a major's cluster. Westfield Center's favorite son Ralph Ward answered to a higher authority than a simple general of the armies when he became a man dedicated to matters of faith so long ago—faith that would be sorely tested as Ralph Ward passed through the hell of Japan's definition of honorable warfare.

It was the Methodist interpretation of Christianity that Ward had always held dear as a young man and then on into adulthood. The calling to the pulpit was never in question, and there was no need to search for convenient deities to worship to justify his own life. It was religion by the book, both the Bible and the tenements of the faith. It was a profession that was a most perfect fit to the young man on a mission.

A master of holy scripture as well as the pulpit, Ralph Ward was also more than capable as a counselor, administrator and anything else a good minister must be. So good in fact that Ward would make the rounds up through the ranks of Methodist hierarchy as he honed his skill as a man of God. Even without personal political agenda, he would be appointed as bishop of the church, but only on a temporary basis. Ralph A. Ward had other things in mind to serve God than watching over Ohio's flocks. He was out to save the entire nation of China.

For thirty-two years, Ward would bring the Good Word through China, to the big cities and the backwoods villages as well. He developed a friendship with a local Methodist, a young man by the name of Chiang Kai-shek, but political maneuverings weren't what had brought the pastor to the Far East. It was all about souls and a life in Christ—a life most in the United States could understand no better than we can grasp the Fourth of July today.

Most Americans of the early twentieth century could spell China, and a slight majority might find it on a map, but the land of dynasties remained a total mystery in every way possible in every other aspect. Far from a best friend to presidents and the economic goliath it is today, China was at best backward and at worst barbarically primitive when the Great Depression struck the world. Divided by internal politics for centuries, invaded at one time or another from every direction, the Mainland seemed a land lost in every respect—just the fertile ground that a missionary could call his home, even when the Japanese came calling.

There was every opportunity to escape, but Reverend Ralph Ward stood his ground as the Rising Sun came from the north. There would always be a soul to save, a sick person to nurse and a spirit to raise. In the middle of January 1942, Ward became another government statistic, a prisoner of war to a nation that did not believe in the Geneva Convention. In reality, he was considered dead, or at least given virtually no chance for survival. Such is the power of true faith—Ralph Ward was about to triumph.

For three and a half years, Bishop Ward remained incarcerated in the most squalid, deplorable conditions on earth. Not once did his belief waver, even as food and water became a premium. Even as those around him went to their eternal rewards, Ward kept the spirit alive. On this day in 1945, that faith received its earthly reward when American GI's tore open the prison camp gates; freedom was at hand, and Ralph Ward fell to his knees to thank God for all his blessings.

Freedom, given by God, the true meaning of the Fourth of July for one, just another of the Greatest almost forgotten to this day. Nearly as forgotten as the oldest man of the sea.

THE OLD MAN OF THE SEA

July 11, 2013

Ed Stoddard would have liked to have gone to the Medina High School reunion that summer of 1943. Not that he had a lot of friends from school days, but it would have been nice to see how everybody had turned out. It was one of those things he'd have to live without though. There was a matter of duty, his Uncle Sam needing him at the moment. Ed Stoddard set off to be another of the truly forgotten veterans of World War II, one of the Merchant Marines.

Long before the nation made it official with declarations, merchant sailors of the United States were well aware that there was a war going on. In 1939, 1940 and throughout 1941, they had run the gauntlet that was both the Atlantic and the Pacific to transport supplies. They'd already suffered losses and casualties from enemy attack well before Pearl Harbor. It was all because the Axis powers understood the basic premise of combat: winning and losing a war is all about supply.

For all the basic and then advanced training, an army without food and supplies never leaves the induction center, let alone sets off to conquer the enemy. That axiom has been true of all militaries for all time, but it never matched the needs of combatants in World War II. Beyond food, uniforms and weapons of war, the needs of this global conflict demanded oil and metal products like never before. It was a concept that the Japanese seemed to grasp instantly.

Even before the invasion of China, long before Pearl Harbor, Imperial Japan knew that there had to be a constant source of supply for its war needs—supplies that must move by ship to an island nation. It was a notion that the Germans understood as well when war broke out with England, not for their own supply but rather to prevent Great Britain from surviving. The finest of warships and submarines set out of ports from Kobe, Osaka and Tokyo to keep supplies flowing. From Hamburg and Kiel, they sailed to sink every ship carrying supplies to the enemy. It was into this world that Ed Stoddard sailed, knowing that there never would be much when it came to reward.

To this day, the United States government has yet to recognize the merchant sailors of World War II as members of the military. In spite of providing essential service without which the war would have been lost long before America entered the fray, the salts of shipping lanes remain civilian employees. No matter how many torpedoes from U-boats they might have dodged or Zeros they avoided, the Merchant Marines were never officially in battle. Injustice wasn't the issue to merchant sailors; it was all about doing the job.

In that world, Ed Stoddard of Medina labored every day throughout World War II. He worked on the dock, carefully loading the supplies into the hold of his ship to balance a load. He cast off when they left the dock, watching carefully as they set to sea. For hours on end, he stood watch, staring into the horizon for the telltale periscope of a German crew that meant to send him and his ship to the bottom. He watched the skies for hurricanes and fighters, hoping that this was another lucky day. When port came into sight, he and all the crew breathed a sigh of relief, knowing that they were about to do it all over again. All in the name of the cause.

The Germans would eventually lose North Africa, not because of battle but the lack of supplies. Thousands of Japanese were starved into surrender or death when their salvation sank to the bottom of the ocean. Not once did Ed Stoddard's cargo fail to make its destination port. A lot of Allied ships never made it home again, but Stoddard did, the old salt serving the duration and serving his nation with not even a letter of discharge when he finally went on the beach. Not even a chance to go to that reunion in the summer of 1943.

Not that there would have been that many old friends at the reunion anyway. Most had already moved on to another life by the summer of '43. They never knew the hero they'd once been in school with so many years before. The old salt who truly was the old man of the sea, seventy-five-year-old Ed Stoddard, class of 1886, another of the unsung heroes of World War II all along the bounding main.

ENERGY-EFFICIENT LIVING

July 25, 2013

It was the latest advancement in geothermal engineering, the ultimate when it came to in-ground living. The most common type of dwelling for officers and enlisted men alike in World War II had nothing to do with energy efficiency though. It was all about staying alive, and we call it the foxhole.

The subterranean abodes were an extension of military strategies of World War I, when months turned into years inside the static lines of trenches across Europe. So fixated on the past was the United States Army that engineering manuals issued during the war prescribed the proper shape and dimensions of a standard foxhole. Measuring six feet across, four feet back to front, four feet deep and with even a ledge dug across the front to aid in firing a rifle, the theory of the manual was to provide a brief respite for the mobile combatant. In reality, it was all a matter of survival.

Alvin Hedrick of Medina learned that in a hurry in 1942 when he set foot on a rock the brass had called Guadalcanal. The entrenching shovel that had been standard issue when he shipped out and a constant pain ever since suddenly became his best friend. Ninety-six cubic feet of dirt never moved so fast as when an infantryman realized that somebody was shooting at him. It might not have been regulation by an engineer's manual, but that was irrelevant. Just as long as it kept Japanese bullets above him, not in him, any hole was going to do. For the boys like Bob Young, those holes were going to become a way of life.

War against the Japanese could be a fluid affair, with islands to be taken and then moving on to the next across the vast expanse of the Pacific Ocean. In Europe after June 6, 1944, it was the slow, unrelenting assault on an opponent more than ready to stand his ground. Battles in France, Holland

and Belgium could be a matter of inches at times. Not trench warfare (but not far from it), the European Theater of operations infantryman often found that his next mailing address was going to be a hole in the ground.

Created for the same reason as they were in the Pacific, European foxholes began in a sense of urgency that only German bullets passing by could instill. Using the same entrenching tool, foxholes first came to the continent on June 6 and stayed for the duration. For soldiers like Bob Young, it was all about making the best of a really bad situation.

Inside that ninety-six cubic feet, two troopers would live nearly twenty-four hours a day. With any luck, the captain would have picked out soft soil for digging someplace near an evergreen forest. Pine boughs made marvelous roofing for foxholes, especially when the Germans insisted on firing shrapnel into the tree branches overhead. One man would sleep, the other would stand watch and the commander would come by every few hours to check on his troops, in a perfect world. After June 6, 1944, there was no perfect world in Europe, though, and most of it had to do with the weather.

Bob Young had already had his share of problems before he dug his first foxhole. He'd managed to come out of the water at Omaha Beach on D-Day and get captured. Shortly afterward, he'd be captured again, this time by Americans who didn't believe that he was a GI when they came across a German patrol taking him back behind the lines. About the first time they dug in for the night, Young was beginning to realize that the climate in Europe wasn't quite like back home in Lodi.

If it wasn't raining, it was snowing—either way, the condensation collected in the bottom of Young's new homes. A poncho wasn't much help, and sitting on a helmet wasn't any better. It was always too wet to start a fire, not that they could. Smoke was a tell-tale giveaway to German artillery spotters. The food was cold, the mail was once a week and there was no glory in being miserable with frostbite or trench foot. There was just a job to do, never thinking about what they were really leaving behind.

To this day, they're still there, holes in the ground by the thousands across Europe and the Pacific. The foxhole, the real monument to who they were—the Bob Youngs, the Alvin Hedricks and the thousands just like them. Permanent memorials even as one bunch of heroes' memorials would never be found.

One They'd All Like to Forget

August 1, 2013

Tom Goff was a lucky man sixty-nine years ago today, and Keith Mantz wasn't—that is a definition of war at its most horrific. Two Medina County boys, one from Homerville and the other from Spencer, who had traveled halfway around the world to serve on the same ship. They both were eyewitnesses to the nation's greatest secret and didn't know it. Together they would be part of the U.S. Navy's most embarrassing moment as well. Two sailors and their ship, the USS *Indianapolis*.

Even though a combat vet and survivor of kamikaze attack, the *Indianapolis* truly began its rise to immortality on July 16, 1945. On that date, it set sail out of San Francisco for Hawaii and then the island of Tinian, carrying its usual crew, a few mysterious passengers and a closely guarded container. Goff and Mantz speculated like everybody else what could be so important inside that wooden box that justified a Marine detachment to stand watch twenty-four hours a day, but they were sailors first. Busy sailors on a cruiser that didn't want to slow down.

Seventy-four and a half hours later, in a record that still stands, the USS *Indianapolis* made port in the Islands. Most of the passengers were let off, but the mysterious cargo and its guards remained. The betting action within the crew was fast and furious as to what was in the box, even as the ship arrived in the Tinian harbor a week later on the morning of July 26, five thousand miles from San Francisco. America's greatest secret, the atomic bomb, had arrived, but only a few on board knew at the moment. Very few of the crew would ever find out. Keith Mantz and more than eight hundred of his shipmates were about to take their last voyage.

There was a war still to be won, with the *Indianapolis* setting sail two days later, headed to the Philippines. An invasion of the mainland of Japan seemed the only military strategy for the time, and there was much preparation before then for every ship of the line. The *Indianapolis* never made it to Leyte Gulf, though—two torpedoes from the Japanese sub *I-58* put it on the bottom of the Pacific in the early morning hours of July 30, 1945. At that moment, the real story begins. The U.S. Navy didn't know the ship was lost.

Sailors had been killed in the explosion and sinking, of that there is no doubt. Many more would die as it took four days for the navy to realize the situation and then to find the survivors; 880 young men perished from explosion, fire, drowning, shark attack, exposure and thirst before rescue came. By August 4, 1945, as the survivors came out of the water, all that was left was to find someone to blame.

For the navy, it was simple: it court-martialed the captain who had survived the sinking, the only commander so punished in the course of the war. The general public saw the matter differently than simple navy blue and gold. Almost immediately, there were questions. Seventy years later, historians are incensed by the cover-ups and vendettas of 1945 that crucified one man to save the reputation and careers of a few others. For Tom Goff, once of the *Indianapolis*, it wasn't about cover-up. It was all a matter of surviving.

Goff didn't care that the commander of the United States Navy had held a grudge against the *Indianapolis*'s skipper for years. It was of no concern that at least half a dozen navy officials had been derelict in their duties, first to warn of potential sub attack and then in commissioning a rescue. All that mattered to the kid from Homerville was that there would be a sunrise on August 3, 1945, and that he'd be alive to see it.

The shipfitter third class turned survivor first class in those four days in sea. Keith Mantz was lost forever, but Tom Goff would make it. He clung to debris, he tread water, he dodged sharks, he questioned if there was a God and then he was saved. He was lucky and Mantz wasn't. Fewer than four hundred survivors—all to deliver a secret cargo that would end the war. A cargo that would hold one last secret for sixty-nine years.

Secret until next week, the one last mystery of the atomic bomb, found right here in little old Medina County, USA.

JUST SOME GUYS DOING THEIR JOBS

August 8, 2013

It is an easy place to miss, this Alloy Fabrication on State Road 83 just southeast of Lodi. At first and second glance, it is another of the small industrial sites here in the county. One-story building, with a sign out front and cars in the parking lot. Unless somebody needs the perfectly formed piece of metal, they pass by without noticing even that. Just the kind of place the United States military had in mind once upon a time.

That time was the late summer of 1944, the day the government came calling to Alloy. The fabrication shop and office were located uptown in

Lodi back then, but everything else was the same. A quality product made to order by craftsmen was the norm then just as it is now. Business owner C.E. Warner listened to the bureaucrats and didn't see much problem, and the job was his. Alloy Fabrication was about to alter the world.

The project itself was actually quite simple by 1944 standards, let alone the high-tech world of today. The government had need of a couple of sets of enclosures made of stainless steel. When assembled, they would be somewhat spherical in shape. Not extremely large, not microscopic, more to the order of nondescript. It was the standards that posed an issue to the average shop in America though. This truly was a production with zero tolerance for error and absolutely no derivation allowed. These standards would be an issue to the ordinary facility, an ordinary run to workers at Alloy Fabrication.

Toward the end of 1944, the job was finished. Mr. Warner was satisfied, and the government inspectors who had stood around taking up space while the shop worked had approved of what they saw. Nobody on the floor who actually did the work gave it much thought; it was just another part for something in the military. They'd seen inspectors before. It was no big thing. Probably a nose cone for a new plane or something like that. Not much to get excited about at all.

With that, the product was put into wooden crates, loaded onto a local delivery truck, taken down to the Lodi train depot and put on a westbound freight train bound for some place called Hanford, Washington. The crates were nothing out of the ordinary, no armed guards watched over every move, no FBI agents lurked in dark shadows and there was absolutely no need for anything when it came to security apparently. It was just another set of crates to be shipped in the name of the war effort. Crates that contained Alloy Fabrication's finest effort, the casings for the atomic bombs.

The uranium and plutonium blockbusters that devastated Hiroshima and Nagasaki were not the war's first weapons of mass destruction but are the most vilified in a politically correct society. The Nazis' gas chambers killed millions. The incendiary bombs in Europe and Japan slaughtered a million more, but it is the atomic bomb that remains the evil tool of good to those who believe that it is possible to reason with the Taliban. To the realists of 1945, the atomic bombs Little Boy and Fat Man were the only option left.

A conventional war had been fought and won in Europe, but an unconventional war raged on in the summer of 1945 in the Pacific. The Japanese had exhibited a lack of what most of the world considered morality from the moment they first attacked China in 1931. There had been poison gas put into use by the Imperial Japanese Army, a total disregard for prisoners' rights, the savage unprovoked attack at Pearl Harbor against the Americans and a total willingness to die for the emperor throughout. Americans cannot understand suicidal dedication to this day, but they understood in 1945 that the Japanese people did.

Japan was perfectly willing to accept that 20 million of its own civilians would die when the Americans invaded the homeland. The nation had already sacrificed hundreds of thousands of its soldiers and sailors without concern. It was a war it could not win. It couldn't even tie, but it was perfectly willing to fight on until American dedication encased in Lodi, Ohio stainless steel fell from the sky.

Peace returned, a war ended, soldiers came home and a small industrial concern kept right on doing the best job it could. It still does today, but now the secret is out. Alloy Fabrications, the guys who won the war one casting and one explosion at a time.

LESSONS FROM THE CHOW LINE

August 15, 2013

"Keep it moving. Get the lead out."

That was the holy mantra of the army cook in World War II. Three times a day, in all kinds of weather, in conditions that defied description and sanity, the troops lined up and passed in review of the stew pots somewhere. Armed with ladles, the cook staff stood for hours dishing out food and taking abuse in return. It was a scene that Wadsworth's Neal Johnson had seen too many times already by the close of 1942.

He'd left the States in October of 1942 to be a combat engineer in the South Pacific. He was supposed to be building bridges and clearing roadways to keep the troops moving—at least by what he was taught and what the book said—the book the Japanese hadn't bothered to read, apparently. Reality made it much more the life of a combat infantryman than engineer. Within just a few months, Johnson had the scar and the stories to prove it.

It was in the Solomons where he got the scar and the Purple Heart that went with every combat wound. It was just a routine patrol; fortunately, a Japanese sniper's aim was a accurate as a weather report seventy years later. Johnson took one in the ankle, a firefight broke out and the squad vanished

More of home: the beautiful girl of every USO show and her boyfriends of the hour. *Diane Bumba Collection.*

somewhere to safer pastures. He ended up crawling two and a half miles back to camp to get out of that mess. It was a ticket stateside for a few weeks to recover, and Johnson made sure that the stories went with him.

Getting wounded on a combat patrol was terrifying but nothing like another outing he'd been on just a few weeks before. Another routine patrol—a few pot shots here and there, and his M-1 had jammed. Johnson was standing there trying to clear it, with the squad moving on, when three Japanese came out of the brush. It was hand to hand, just like they had taught in Basic. The weapon was a club, the bayonet was a trench knife and three Japanese families were left to mourn. It had been terrifying too, but nothing like the ultimate fright. That one came one day in the chow line.

It was on Guadalcanal, the site of the first American amphibious invasion of World War II. The Marines had done the dirty work for three long, bloody months at the cost of horrific casualties. When November 1942 came, it was the army's turn to mop up and secure as the Marines shipped out to refit in Australia. There was still action, but most of the construction work could go on without too much of a hitch. Just the kind of place a combat engineer would fit right in.

The outdoor theater at every installation of the Pacific. Movies under the stars and, once in a while, the stars themselves, like Bob Hope. *Diane Bumba Collection.*

Fit in so much that the first few months of Neal Johnson's overseas deployment very quickly became a matter of routine. There was the airfield to get totally operational and then buildings to be put up. Command post or quarters, it made no difference to the masters of hammer and nail. Occasionally, the Japanese still on the island would make things interesting, but it was a war after all—a war where Johnson even learned how to pick out a chow line.

It is a basic fact of military life: if Cookie is a fat slob, you stand in line and wait; the food will be fine. If it's a bunch of skinny runts running mess call, you find someplace else. A man who won't eat a lot of his own cooking just can't be trusted if he's wearing olive drab. It was the fat man's chow line Johnson was in that day on the Canal, shuffling along, figuring the food would be fine, not really thinking about much at all when life suddenly got very interesting.

Cookie slapped a ladle full of something onto the tray as a thought came to Johnson. He was about to comment something to the effect that he'd once stepped in something like this but had never eaten it when Cookie pulled out a .45 automatic and shot the trooper beside Johnson right between the eyes. The cook hadn't gone crazy to an insult. One Wadsworth boy realized that he wasn't such a good trooper after all.

Neal Johnson, combat engineer, combat trooper, had been standing beside a Japanese infiltrator dressed like a GI the whole time he'd been in the chow line. Just another real-life story from another real GI trying to grow up with both feet on the ground while another had other ideas.

GROWING UP ABOVE

August 22, 2013

He was just a kid, barely out of his teens by the time his first career ended. Everett Perkins of Wadsworth never got to know what immaturity felt like, at least by today's definition of cranking up the stereo and saying stupid things to be cool. His coming of age was at thirty thousand feet. He became a man at three hundred miles per hour, living in a world where life expectancies were measured in days. His first real job was the top turret gunner in a B-17 during World War II.

The B-17 was a creation of the Boeing Company back in 1935. Unlike 2012 thinking about the future in technology, the plane was financed by private and not public money. The government saw little need for a long-range bomber, in its infinite wisdom ready to consign the product to coastal defenses until the world came to its senses. The Boeing Company saw that world differently, realistically, and built itself a masterpiece.

Nearly seventy-five feet long and more that one hundred feet wide at the wing tips, the B-17 weighed in at about the same tonnage as today's fully loaded eighteen wheeler. It had a top speed just over 300 miles per hour, a range of 1,800 miles and a seven-thousand-pound payload to deliver on demand. For its crew of ten, there was none better.

Perk Perkins understood that it would be perfect, no matter what ship assigned to for that day's mission. It is perhaps one of the misperceptions of World War II that bomber crews and their plane were one, an unchanging unit. In actuality, it was more often potluck for crews, especially newer ones, sent off over enemy skies in whatever was available. Such was the greatness of the B-17—it would always be magnificent no matter the serial number.

Up front in the cockpit sat the old man, the pilot who might have reached the age of twenty-five by the time he took control. The best and the brightest of flight trainings and schools, he was the ultimate authority on board, but he knew that it was all a matter of teamwork. The copilot to his right was literally his right-hand man, ready to take over in any situation. It was the other eight crewmen, though, who made the difference between success and death.

Beneath and in front of the cockpit was the navigator's desk and toggler's station. The navigator got them home and back, and the toggler watched the lead ship of the formation, looking for their bombardier to send the signal; then he would send the payload on its way over the target. Then about all they could do was hope that the other six wouldn't have to do their jobs.

There was the flight engineer, in charge of all emergencies that could possibly happen on board. The radio man, with his own machine gun above him as he monitored all the transmissions from command. Left and right waist gunners were ready to take on any attack from the sides, and then there was the smallest of the crew, the little one who crawled back the tunnel to his cave as the tail gunner. Then there were the Everett Perkins of the Army Air Corps.

At thirty thousand feet inside a Plexiglas turret, he waged war every second the ship was in the air. The battlefield was 360 degrees on the horizontal, 180 degrees to the vertical, where the enemy might well be visible for only a few seconds if at all. It was enough to drive any airman insane, but Perk Perkins battled on inside a thin sheet of Plexiglas where the outside temperatures reached fifty-five below zero. It was the life of the turret gunner, the Japanese pilots' most tempting target on the Flying Fortress over the South Pacific.

It was late 1942 when the Wadsworth kid who had been an eyewitness to Pearl Harbor was confirmed as the hero he truly was in the skies over Rabaul. Three separate decorations for bravery and one Purple Heart, but to Perkins, it was just a matter of doing his job—doing the right thing, that day and every day that came after long after he left his sheepskin flying suit, flak vest, helmet and electric gloves behind. Then he could get on with that second career: running a hardware store.

Just another of the Greatest it's only taken seventy years to recognize from right here in little old Medina County, USA.

Then Comes Transition

August 29, 2013

No doubt about it: the illness has arrived. It first showed up about a year ago, but the symptoms passed in a day or two. It came back with a gusto a few weeks back when they buried today's story over at Western Reserve National Cemetery. This isn't Parkinson's or whatever it is that is making things inconvenient at times around our house. We'll figure that out some other time. This one is for sure—I've come down with a case of Ernie Pyle Disease.

Ernie Pyle, the greatest war correspondent ever. There isn't a journalist who covers conflict who doesn't want to be compared to the little guy, but nobody ever will equal the master. He paid his dues in the front line of World War II Europe, making it real and making the average dogface immortal. He kept "I" out of the equation, something that today's columnists have forgotten. It was all about the ordinary GI. Eventually, he gave his life for the story, but there was something about Pyle often forgotten. Right in the middle of it all, he had to stop.

The disadvantage of war is that good kids die. At a certain point, it stops being a story and becomes personal. Even the great Pyle had to step back and regroup after one too many of his boys didn't make it back. Regroup and do a few other things, knowing that time would figure it all out. Ernie Pyle Disease—when it stops being reporting the story and one starts feeling those things called emotions.

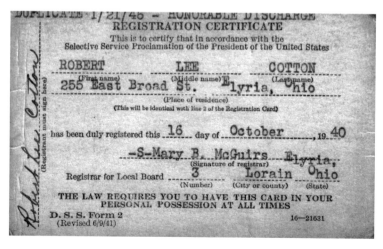

Then there was this, the golden ticket, the right to go home. The war was over.
Diane Bumba Collection.

The disadvantage of real life is that great old men die too. Men who became friends, happy that somebody was willing to hear the story they were finally ready to tell. It got personal, a modest man who didn't care about being immortal, just as long as somebody listened and might understand what once was real. The playing of Taps the other day over at Western Reserve made a good excuse to consider a few other things. He was one the world will miss every day.

This column began a few years ago, taking a look at Medina County during the American Civil War. The *Gazette*, thanks to George Hudnutt, was the only newspaper in the entire nation to run a weekly commemorating the 150th anniversary of that national tragedy. After a year, we moved on to the Greatest.

For eighteen months, each week covered that generation and the incredible contributions this little place called Medina County made to literally saving the world. There's still another two years of stories, just not now. Whether or not anybody understood the point remains to be seen.

It's about those people and places that should give us a great sense of community pride with some college-level history thrown in as well. It's a

Faith, even when a soldier might feel so alone, is never far from sight.
National Archives and Records Administration, Benson Collection, 111-SC-188691.

145

bonus if anybody has caught that history is just the past tense of the present. The stupidity of today is nothing new—no matter where stupid is found. We simply repeat the past until we finally find a solution, knowing that we'll foul it up again and have to start over. We're Americans. We do that well.

The whole concept, Civil War or World War II, has been so incredibly enjoyable. The egotist does like to hear that his work is read, and the historian is pleased that his stories will live forever. It would be nice to keep it all at a distance, but Taps, born in the Civil War and still alive today, was the call to do something else for a while.

Not stop, just something else. Similar and yet completely different. We did the Civil War and then World War II. Perhaps it's time to split the difference and turn 180 degrees. To look somewhere in the period between 1870 and 1900. To search out not the heroes but the other side of humanity. We've done the Uncivil War for two and a half years. Now it's time to do Uncivil Medina, and trust me, we had the characters to make a play and then fill a book.

Interesting characters like the former county prosecutor and bank executive who ended his life doing life without parole in North Dakota. The housewife who spent ten years in the Ohio Penitentiary for a murder that never happened. The most despicable man in county history, who committed suicide only with a sheriff's help. Our inglorious ancestors we hope we're not related to and will fascinate us so. People like the human chameleon W.W. Pancoast...but that's a story to be told another time and in another book.

Part III

EVER AFTER

THE LAST BATTLE OF WORLD WAR II

July 19, 2012

Her name will be Sue, no other identifier being necessary for our purposes. Given the situation, there should be a certain degree of privacy granted. In spite of the sparkling eyes and radiance that shows wherever she goes, there is a veneer to it all. Truth be known, Sue and thousands of other women across America have an issue most will hopefully never have to deal with in their lives. These women are fighting the last battle of World War II. Their veteran fathers have Alzheimer's disease.

Once upon a time, he was just another tall, skinny kid of Medina County. A prominent family background and a local road named in one ancestor's honor. Without Pearl Harbor, it's hard to say how he would have matured or what he would have been, but the war changed all that. As soon as he was able, he was off to serve the nation as just another dogface. Just an ordinary GI who ended up making good.

It was in the forgotten theater of U.S. Army operations that he would earn his stripes. Most of the casual scholars of the conflict today assume that the South Pacific was a navy and Marine operation and the European front reserved for the army. In fact, at dozens of islands across the Pacific, there would be joint assaults by all three branches of the service. What the Marines took, the army held and then vice versa a few

Once upon a time, the old men of today were just kids trying so hard to be brave. Diane Bumba Collection.

months later. It was across those sandbars and coral reefs that the skinny kid became a man.

He never got much mention in the local paper during the war—just an occasional sentence about a promotion. One stripe and then the second. Before long it was "Sarge," but he wasn't there for promotions. Just another trooper doing his job, wanting to get it over. Get it won and then coming home to build a life, marry his sweetheart, raise his children and live happily ever after. Happy until the illness came calling.

I ate dinner with the Sarge a few months ago at a local community event. We hadn't seen each other in several years, more turnings of the calendar than I want to admit now. I didn't catch it at first, as I was just happy to visit and enjoy the day. About the second time he asked me the same question, I understood quite well the minefield that I'd walked into. It was a good day for him; he remembered me well but not what we'd just eaten. We talked of Basic even if he did insist that I was there too. Best to go along—the great disadvantage of fighting an enemy who takes no prisoners.

Whether it be dementia, senility or Alzheimer's, there is no more frustrating illness for the surviving family than when the mind begins to fade faster than the body. Those like myself who have dealt with it understand. Those who have not have my constant hope that they will never. Those who deal with it now have my total, complete admiration. They were the Greatest once upon a time, and nothing, not even this, should ever diminish our admiration and total respect for each and every one. We will not win this battle, but we will survive even better.

Sharing these type of experiences that Sue now lives is just one of the projects of a new organization coming together in Medina County. Chartered by the State of Ohio as a heritage group, the Daughters of World War II will be locating its headquarters here. Although it is not about jobs or economic prosperity, at least not yet, the noble cause does seem to be a right and decent thing. We will be home to an organization that has a mission into eternity.

Established with the purpose that the Greatest Generation should not be allowed to fade away, the Daughters of World War II will be open to any woman who is a descendant of World War II veterans, Merchant Marines or Essential Civilian Workers. They are out to discover who Dad or Mom really were and make sure that the next generation knows the story as well. Somewhere along the way, I strongly suspect that they will even help fight that last battle with Sue and others just like her, one way or another.

It does seem like the right thing to be here, in the place that gave so much, little old Medina County, USA.

IN A VERY SMALL WORLD

September 27, 2012

The great actor George Kennedy had a good reason to be cast as an officer in *The Dirty Dozen*, having been on Patton's staff in World War II. Donald Pleasance had some expertise before he began filming *The Great Escape*, having been a prisoner of war in Germany during 1945. No matter which direction you care to look, some of the most famous people of entertainment in the twentieth century happened to have been some of the Greatest Generation. It makes today's society almost marvel at how little we admire.

Instead of whining about social issues and getting the public's hopes up by threatening to migrate, Hollywood royalty at the start of World War II took another approach to a national crisis. They stepped up and got involved.

Gone with the Wind star Clark Gable had no qualms at all at becoming a waist gunner on a B-17 over Europe after his beloved Carole Lombard was killed during a stateside bond drive. His co-star Leslie Howard gave his life in the cause of the British Secret Service, while Maurice Chevalier fought with the French Resistance. The list is almost endless of celebrity contributions in the name of their nation.

The original Uncle Fester of the Addams Family, Jackie Coogan, was a glider pilot in the Pacific, at one time flying over the headquarters of Anti-Submarine Unit 1139, where a kid named Kirk Douglas was a communications officer. Just offshore aboard the carrier *Lake Champlain*, his counterpart was a young man named Jack Lemmon. Not far away, an absent-minded mechanic named Rock Hudson caused two cargo planes to collide on the runway in spite of all the training he'd received from Lieutenant Robert Taylor stateside. Lee Marvin was a combat Marine, and Captain Kangaroo was not a captain but rather was so much more. Just a scratch on the surface of the contributions in the cause of a nation by the soon-to-be-famous.

Halfway around the world from the Pacific, a sketch artist named Dirk Bogarde captured the scenes of Normandy on board an assault ship as movie villain Neville Brand would become the fourth-most-decorated soldier in U.S. Army history. A tall kid named James Arness took a leg wound on the beach at Anzio, while a dogface called Tony Bennett carried a pack through bocage country. High above one of the best gunners of the U.S. Army Air Corps was a young man named Walter Matthau. One of the most daring commandos of the war was Douglas Fairbanks Jr., whose accomplishments pale in comparison to an OSS operative in Yugoslavia named Sterling Hayden. Courage to the point of craziness, just like a combat engineer who spent the Battle of the Bulge disarming land mines, a little guy named Mel Brooks.

Even the ranks stateside would carry a fair share of names soon to be unforgettable. Captain Ronald Reagan processed discharge paperwork on the West Coast, while a Coast Guard sailor named Sid Caesar patrolled the docks of New York. A short distance away in an office building, the radio announcer for broadcasts into Occupied France was Yul Brynner. North of the border, a stocky Welshman named Richard Burton took flight training between happy hours. Famous people in an immortal cause no matter which way you looked.

John Buchanan and Larry Newberry of Medina figured that some day they'd get a chance to see some of those famous people of Hollywood. The two buddies managed to get to Basic together out in New Mexico. With any luck, they'd be fliers. With a lot of luck, they'd get leave to Hollywood, visit that Stage Door Canteen and maybe even see Myrna Loy. One thing for sure, though: they definitely would take Jim with them.

A good guy, this Jim, so skinny they almost didn't let him in the service. Awful quiet though, not much for boozing and babes. A lot more dedicated to training than most too, but then again, he wanted a career out of flying. The guys from Medina never did make it to meet Myrna, but Jim sure did get a future in the air.

By the time Jim retired, he had made it all the way to brigadier general in the United States Air Force. A smart kid, having a career in case his day job didn't work out. In the end, both careers did, with gold stars and gold statutes. The nice guy, brigadier general and film star Jimmy Stewart, pal to a couple of guys who came home to a lot of stories. Stories not everyone will ever choose to tell.

WHEN NO STORY IS THE STORY

January 31, 2013

"It is good war is so terrible, lest we grow too fond of it."

Those words were spoken on a cold December day in 1862 by Confederate General Robert E. Lee as he watched the slaughter in front of him at the Battle of Fredericksburg, Virginia. No truer syllables were ever uttered, no military adage ever greater. Yet for all our study in war colleges and military academies, it is a situation that has been and will be repeated. A situation whose reality only some will ever comprehend.

If we as scholars of the past were not there physically on the scene, we will never understand what truly happened. It is easy to look back at events altered by hazy fields and hazier memories, but we only see concepts. We do not capture the real stories of the terror or inhumanity of war by looking at reports. Human emotions under stress are much harder to get to surrender to our quest for knowledge. It is the great disadvantage in trying to carry on what Ernie Pyle once mastered, to bring home the stories of the hometown kids who fought in World War II. Sometimes you just have to let it go.

So it will be for another of the true heroes of World War II who came from Medina. Once upon a time, he was a good kid, just a teenager full of promise. Today, he is one of the wise seniors. In that time between, in the caldron that was World War II, he was forced to be something else, another

The result when all the shooting stopped: lovers again, lovers forever. *Diane Bumba Collection.*

person he didn't want to be, a battle-hardened soldier. He today would prefer never to speak of it, a situation I well understand. What he did must never be forgotten.

They were all boys who formed up that rifle platoon in K Company when they first set out. By the end of Basic, they had become dogfaces, the ground-pounding, mud-slogging, constantly complaining infantry who would win the war one foxhole at a time. About three yards into France, they all became men, fighting at the broken end of a bottle across Europe. Then there was that day in early 1945.

Somewhere in all the military archives, there is buried an official account of what happened in January at Julich, Germany. To one kid from Medina, it's not important; he was just doing his job. The captain gave him a medal, they all said that he did a good job and then K Company headed out again, four more months of war waiting to be finished. Four more months in the hell of 1945 Germany that we of this time cannot even begin to imagine.

There are no civilian casualties to a five-hundred-pound bomb dropped from ten thousand feet—just targets to be destroyed. From two miles above, killing becomes sanitary, and yet to the infantryman who walks through the result, humanity becomes a jumble of body parts, not personalities. Perhaps they had been Nazis, perhaps not; the only consolation was that they had supported the enemy in some way. The only hope was that it might all end tomorrow.

There is no collateral damage to a 76mm tank shell—just a communications center or machine gun nest destroyed. The sacred ground that might have stood beside it for ten centuries becomes an irrelevant pile of rubble in total war. Another objective achieved, one more step closer to finishing the slaughter and going home. Matters of faith or historical importance bear no meaning to a dogface passing by. By the very end, neither did life to some human beings.

There is no logic in fanatics who refuse to surrender while surrounded by carnage. They were the Werewolves, some not even teenagers, the last gasp of true Nazism, who gave up their lives for one last shot at a victor. Children were dying because they had been indoctrinated by idiots now dead themselves, and the dogfaces saw it all. They saw it and cannot forget it.

Those of us in the next generations cannot imagine, for all our newsreels, for all our Military Channels, for all our movies, and therefore it is pointless for us to try to understand. My silent friend, that Bronze Star they gave you is not enough. With the disadvantage of not comprehending, I don't know how to say thanks. The best I can do is appreciate you, just another dogface, just another of the Greatest from a time so many of us might never understand.

THOSE BRAVE, MODEST MEN

March 7, 2013

If it wasn't so stupid, it would have been outright funny. After a lecture on photographic interpretation down in Columbus, one of the attendees approached me with the novel concept that I should write about him. I looked at the photo he gave me and remembered that Dad always taught me to be polite. The image showed my new friend in a unique interpretation of western wear, sitting atop what we would have called a plow nag down home. According to his story, I was talking to the last cowboy to cross the Broad Street Bridge in the capital city. I just smiled and wondered what Sid or Junior would have said.

Sid Meager of Seville and Junior Woodruff from Medina were old-school kind of guys. Part of that bygone generation that believed that the only time a man's name should appear in the newspaper was when he was born, when he got married and when he died. Any other news other than a vital statistic was usually not for something good or all a matter of ego. Sid and Junior were no egotists, but they didn't achieve the objective of remaining anonymous either. Each name managed to slip into the *Gazette* once during World War II. It was the high cost of being the hero one time and then doing it again.

It is the Silver Star, the nation's third-highest award for heroism under fire. It is a subjective award but an honor that is never presented lightly. For every recommendation for the Silver Star during the war, only one in ten were

A happy-go-lucky corporal who would win two Silver Stars by tempting death every day overseas far beyond the front lines. *Kurjian Family Archives.*

bucked up channels for consideration. Of the ones that made the cut, only one in ten would survive investigation and be awarded. One award out of one hundred submissions are not good odds. Just about the same odds Sid Meager had to survive.

In theory, it is a simple concept: an artillery piece is aimed in the right direction, set for a certain distance and fired, the projectile it launches therefore landing right on target. In actuality, there are a thousand variables that enter into the equation to land that missile of death anywhere near the intended target and only one solution to make sure it all turns out right. The solution was called the forward observer, and their lives bordered on absolute insanity.

Carrying a rifle and a radio, forward observers like Sid Meager were sent out beyond Allied lines toward the Germans to watch where artillery shells fell. Calling back over the radio, they would adjust direction and distance for the cannons that could be a mile or more behind them. In the 276th Armored Field Artillery, duty like Meager's generally involved a life expectancy of minutes, not years, once the Germans had spotted him. Bordering on certain death at least three times, Sid Meager had continued to direct fire as he attempted to hold off the enemy all across the drive to the Rhine. In the end, it was worth two Silver Stars, his heroic achievement nothing more than pure luck, at least by his estimation. When it came to Junior Woodruff, it was more a matter of divine intervention.

The hand of God is the only way Captain Woodruff could explain the fact any of them survived that time in hell during World War II. He'd earned his first Silver Star the first day it all broke loose; the cluster then went with it just a few days later when it looked like the end of the world was at hand. There was absolutely no logical explanation why the Germans hadn't killed every one of them. There was even less logic in the fact the Americans were actually winning the battle, driving Hitler's boys back when the glory hounds came crashing in to grab the headlines.

At least that's how Captain Woodruff saw it. They had everything under control. They didn't need any help, but bigger brass saw it differently. Especially the guy named Patton who came up from the south, led by a forward observer named Meager with the 3rd Army, which came crashing into Woodruff's foxhole at a place called Bastogne in a little thing called the Battle of the Bulge.

Two hometown American heroes, four Silver Stars between them, both in the same foxhole, and some idiot wanted me to write about a pretend cowboy. Oh well, it was Columbus, a long way from the home of heroes and sanity, little old Medina County, USA.

All the Treasures in the Attic

March 14, 2013

It's Exasperation Television, the current glut of historical experts on the air seeking out America's lost valuables. The one good thing the Antiques Roadshow had has long been corrupted. Now it's all about making the maximum amount of money off the unsuspecting without any regard to true preservation. It makes me wonder what will become of the incredible relics in the attics and basements of Medina County once we realize what they are.

The great advantage to having been a museum curator and a State of Ohio Distinguished Scholar of History is knowing that those artifacts are out there. The great disadvantage to a past like that is to have to watch the television idiots mishandle items as they put a price tag on priceless. To fear that selfish greed will one day be the buzzword of history. There simply is no dollar sign on finding out exactly who our ancestors really were, and hundreds of us have the chance to do that right now.

My B.W. recently began a project to do exactly that, transcribing her uncle's letters home from World War II. Here are the great artifacts of that late unpleasantness, not a uniform or a weapon rather but the writings of those who were there in the messages they sent back to loved ones. For years, these letters had been stowed away, the writing and the uncle fairly well forgotten. Slowly but surely, in his own handwriting, a most amazing veteran's story unfolded.

He was just another eighteen-year-old kid who reported to Great Lakes in 1942, sending back the obligatory first-day postcard of every new recruit.

Long before it became inconvenient to fly, there was only one real way to travel America. *Diane Bumba Collection.*

Within a few weeks, it was postmarks from Florida and then Mississippi, a young man off to something called the Seabees. The military didn't always make sense to him, but neither did some of his letters home, written with a noticeable lack of education. Not that it was going to matter. Within two months, the return address on his envelopes was a place called Guadalcanal.

Much to the chagrin of casual researchers, these letters and thousands like them are not eyewitness accounts of monumental battles. Thanks to training and military censors, the writing seems mundane, almost boring. The weather was warm, they were keeping busy and a sailor couldn't find a decent drink anywhere. Cross-referencing to history and the Seabee was thinking about beer while the Imperial Japanese Navy was coming down the Slot dropping shells on him every night. It takes a little research, but putting it all together will be well worth the hunt to see what really was important to those to whom we owe so much.

The Seabee wished for a beer as he secured Henderson Field. He hoped that everybody had a good Christmas as he leveled out the ground at Vella Lavella so Pappy Boyington could earn a Congressional Medal of Honor. He served the duration and only had one sentence of one letter edited out in the name of security. All those letters tell the story of a kid growing up, a three-year process of becoming a man, and now, even as he is gone, we know him well at last. For our friend Saundra, her artifacts ended up being more a matter of how it all came to be.

The man who would one day be her father was just another Marine on Guadalcanal when the first letter came. A college girl at Kent who one day would be Saundra's mother was doing her patriotic duty, writing to some brave trooper overseas. They'd never met, they probably never would, but it gave a grunt something to do when the Japanese weren't shooting at him. Letters continued to and from Peleliu, Tarawa, Iwo and Okinawa. Letters that eventually seemed to have nothing to do with beer or Christmas wishes.

That tough Marine stayed on duty after the Japanese surrender, assigned occupation duty in Mainland China. It wasn't until June 14, 1946, before he finally got back to Ohio. Back to finally meet this cute college girl and say thank you. The rest is just living history.

Happy sixty-sixth birthday tomorrow, Saundra. You indeed are quite the researcher, as well as a gracious, elegant lady, especially with a blush of discovery. June 14, 1946. July. August. September. October. November. Oops. Oh my, oh my.

The treasures in the attic. Love letters from strangers—yes, they even thought about that in the middle of a war, no matter how saintly they would be for the rest of their lives.

The One Battle Begun So Long Ago

May 9, 2013

It is a war that we will win in the near future, the campaign to exterminate that ultimate evil, tobacco. Whether it is by taxation, medical education or advertising to appeal to morality, this is a crusade bound for victory. With any luck, we can blow enough smoke to forget how we're losing the real war, the one on drugs. We'll deal with concepts for the moment and not worry about details. Instead, let us all congratulate ourselves on how far we've come from seventy years ago, when smokes were king.

Even though tobacco could be considered the first treasure brought back by explorers of the New World, it remained a male vice for the first two and a half centuries of American exploration. Primarily enjoyed to its fullest by the bowlful or by the hand-rolled cigar, the tobacco industry and all of the nation began to change in the closing months of the American Civil War. Using nitrated paper from the Sharps carbine ammunition and a few shreds of loose herb, the cigarette was born. It would take another sixty years of development, but the great evil was loose, and society would eventually be its victim.

By the 1920s, when America had outlawed liquor, the thin white cylinders of tobacco had infiltrated every corner of the nation. It was not only socially acceptable for men as well as women, it was also socially expected to be a smoker. As advertising discovered radio and then the movies, surveys proved that four out of five doctors preferred one brand, while most of Major League Baseball preferred another. By 1940, nearly three-quarters of all American adults enjoyed tobacco in one form or another, even as the government was just then beginning to link health issues with the plant's use. It was a study that got pushed aside on December 7, 1941, for a higher calling. America was suddenly out to save the world, one cigarette at a time.

Once the United States military stopped reeling from Pearl Harbor and began its assault toward victory, one truth became rapidly self-evident. Wherever an American serviceman went, his greatest calling card was an American cigarette. The blends of Virginia and North Carolina tobacco fields opened every door and became a universal currency that today's Euro could only dream of becoming. It was the greatest of trade bait and quickest way to meet that pretty little French girl too. Chewing gum was nice and chocolate bars were fine, but for an American cigarette, natives from North Africa to New Guinea would be a friend for life.

Millions of smokers addicting tens of millions of displaced persons seems like such a moral crime today that we can hardly imagine our insensitivities in 1943. At that moment, a dogface infantryman would probably shrug at our constant need to reform other people's habits. Beyond any doubt, the cigarette dangling off his lip could cause cancer or heart disease in twenty, thirty or forty years. To a trooper who was lucky enough to survive the German barrage just a few minutes before while his buddy didn't, twenty or forty years really didn't matter. It is life for the moment to a combat trooper, a cigarette being that moment's enjoyment. It was an enjoyment that the American people were going to make sure was always going to be available.

Long before astute politicians realized that exploiting smokers was an easy way to finance baseball stadiums, there were no taxes on tobacco products in this nation. A carton of smokes, ten packs, cost a serviceman fifty-nine cents. An entire carton, and it was just over half a buck. The original four-pack was not imported beer but rather those cigarettes packed into every ration box for field troops. In one little backwater, they even went further to make sure that the American way of smoking was always going to be there when the boys needed a light.

They called it Smokes for Yanks, a charity drive that had the sole purpose of buying up cartons of cigarettes and shipping them off, not to the locals but to any serviceman. It was a random mailing, boxes headed off to a general delivery—whoever got there first picked up the Old Golds, Chesterfields, Lucky Strikes or the treasured Camels. More than five thousand cartons were shipped, and almost every one was acknowledged with a note of gratitude from a dogface somewhere.

Dogfaces across the globe who liked this Smokes for Yanks program, born in someplace called little old Medina County, USA.

Like Grains of Sand

May 23, 2013

Words do not consecrate ground to be holy. Only the deeds of those who can no longer speak for themselves will do that. This nation established that at Gettysburg once upon a time. A short distance away from those hallowed grounds of the Civil War, down on Jefferson Davis Highway in Triangle, Virginia, the Marine Memorial Foundation carries on that concept at a place where silence speaks louder than any word ever will.

It is Semper Fidelis Park, a memorial garden associated with the United States Marine Corps Museum, 135 acres of ground that have been dedicated to what is the legacy of the great men and women who always will be the Corps. No interpretive plaques or guides are necessary on this piece of real estate to understand the message here. It is truly all about Semper Fi.

Memorial Day lives here every day of the year, not as the start of summer but as a moment of remembrance. Sixteen thousand inscribed paving stones have been purchased by Marine families to immortalize loved ones here. From this nation's inception all the way through to the military morass we find ourselves in today, Marines have been there. This is grounds for them but a message for all of us as well. There's more than stones or the chapel to be found on the grounds. Every so often, there is a most holy consecration.

Just before Christmas last year, I visited the museum and the accompanying park. The repository of artifacts is excellent, although I wouldn't grant a few

The war was almost over. Time for a dogface and his pup to relax. *Kurjian Family Archives.*

of the staff members such accolades. Perhaps drawing a paycheck is more important than historical interpretation, but the point is inconsequential. They do not represent the majority of the employees or the Corps in any way. It is simply too bad that such petty bureaucrats will never truly understand the scene that unfolded in front of me at Semper Fidelis Park just a short time later.

He was the right age to have seen it all firsthand, the elderly gentleman well ahead of me on the walkway. Once upon a time, he'd been the heartthrob; now the years almost bent him double. The legs that once might have run a marathon needed a cane to walk just a hundred yards. No infirmity mattered, not this day. A solitary man was best left to his solitary memories. There was an old debt to be repaid.

Perhaps he'd once saluted Chippewa Lake's Major John Murray when they were on the Canal. It could have been that he was near Wadsworth's Sandy Doccolo when the craft hit the beach at Saipan and time became no more. Maybe he was with York Township's Emil on the shore at Iwo or saw Medina's Lou Lowery actually take the picture now almost forgotten. He was there somewhere, sometime—of that there was no doubt as I watched him take out a small bag of sand and sprinkle it on one particular brick. I knew I was in the presence of a real Marine.

By the code of honor, he still lived like every Jarhead should—that if a Marine ever returned to that hell that was Iwo Jima, the only thing he would take away from the visit would be some sand. Sand that had been filled once upon a time with Marine Corps blood. Holy sand earned in a way far too many will never comprehend. The old fellow and I never spoke, but we didn't have to. His mission was accomplished, and he didn't need my help. Perhaps our mission now has just begun.

Memorial Day was created to honor the fallen of the Civil War. The holiday was supposed to have died out with the passing of the last veteran of that war, but we have made it into something else. Contrary to what the media tells us, it is not another Veterans' Day or an excuse to cook ribs at fairgrounds. It now should be a time to recall those who gave all in military service. Our way of holding on to memories one more year. For a couple of bucks, we could make some of those we remember immortal. Perhaps someday one of our grandchildren's children will sprinkle holy sand on the names of John, Sandy, Emil or Lou and never forget.

It's not why the boys joined the Corps, but it is what they deserve. Every Marine from everywhere. Semper Fi then, now and forever.

LONG TIME TO RECOVER A SOUVENIR

June 20, 2013

High Holy Weekend of motor sports is upon us now. Each June, they gather at Le Sarthe in France to wage mechanical war at the 24 Hours of Le Mans. More than a car race, it's nationalism at two hundred miles per hour. Once it was the English and their Jaguars who ruled the world, and then the Prancing Horse of Italy took the crown. The Americans made their brief appearance before the Germans returned with the panzers of Porsche. Now it is the latest generation of Auto Union and the Japanese who battle for domination on grounds Medina's Lester Aufmuth knew all so well.

It wasn't as a race fan that the handsome young man saw the area though. No evidence exists that Lieutenant Aufmuth ever witnessed an auto race, let alone this one. His view of Le Mans wasn't from a grandstand on the Muslanne Straight; it was from fifteen thousand feet above back in 1943. Behind the controls of his B-17, Aufmuth was on a mission to holy grounds one flight at a time.

In the early days of World War II, Le Mans was a marshalling yard for German forces in Europe. Men and supplies for every branch of service traveled by rail in those days. Industrial plants and induction centers would forward their products to a central location like Le Mans, with the goods and men distributed to the front from there. Long trains of explosives or infantrymen made most tempting targets. Unfortunately, so too did the American B-17s.

Weighted down by payloads and on fixed paths to the target, the American airships were slow-moving convoys over the skies of France on their way to Le Mans. Below, the Germans had three years to perfect their antiaircraft positions. The Axis air forces held dominion over the skies at the time. For all its attributes and all its armor, the B-17s were far too easy a prey once upon a time in the war.

Lester Aufmuth was well aware of the risks every time he climbed into the cockpit of his ship that summer and fall of 1943. Ever since the very first mission of the U.S. Army Air Corps, far too many planes and their crews hadn't even made it to the target, let alone get back. Even when he did get through, Aufmuth knew that things still didn't always work out as planned. Too many of those five-hundred-pound bombs he'd carried to the target weren't detonating on impact. It seemed like it was all a matter of luck. Aufmuth's luck ran out in September 1943.

It could have been ack-ack, or it might have been an Me109—not that it mattered. Somewhere near Le Mans that day, Lieutenant Aufmuth's plane was hit. The crew all got out as the ship went down, their combat war now over. It would be another twenty months inside a POW compound before Aufmuth saw freedom again, one of thousands first Missing in Action and then Captured, according to the government's records. He'd get home in the end after the camp was liberated, marry his sweetheart and get on with living; he'd never know that a little bit of Lieutenant Aufmuth just might well have stayed behind.

Sports car racing returned to Le Mans soon after the war had ended in Europe. As it did, the legends of this holy ground would be created. The Great Crash of '55. The Cobra Wars of the early 1960s. Wyer's long tail 917s of the early '70s. The 962s of the '80s. The Silver Arrows of the '90s. Great drivers and greater cars going faster and farther each year. For more than sixty years, they have raced and made history, never knowing at the moment how incredibly lucky they all had been.

They found out just a few years ago. After years of events, the track owners at Le Mans finally decided to upgrade some of the grounds. While resurfacing the racetrack beyond pit road, on the grade up to the Dunlop Bridge, not far from the old rail yards, workmen uncovered an unexploded five-hundred-pound bomb from World War II. Two years later, they found another one nearby. Bombs that forensic historians now think to have been left behind by B-17s in the late summer months of 1943.

Just another bomb or two that didn't go off, dropped by just another pilot, just another of the Greatest leaving a contribution even to this day.

No Grave Should Hold Them Down

November 8, 2012

They are nearly a full division strong now, but no barracks mark their camp. Nearly every day, another trooper joins up, but there will be no drill for the ranks. There are no uniforms issued and no equipment to be accounted for. No forced marches, no chow hall and no more battles, not for this elite outfit. They are the World War II veterans interred at the National Cemetery here in Medina County.

It is a sobering site, the acres of flatland off Rawiga Road that now are the final home to so many. This is the one thing our former tenant Sherrod

Brown really got right, as he was instrumental in establishing the hallowed ground. In stark simplicity, there is a great tribute to every single veteran who has gone before. It is indeed a place for great reflection, especially when thoughts turn to those who aren't there.

Medina County's Frank Repp isn't buried at the National Cemetery and never will be. They never found enough of him to bury after a German 88mm vaporized his Sherman tank in Italy. Alec Kukich won't be here either, since the plane he piloted is still somewhere in the South Pacific. Perhaps it is in the sea or somewhere in the jungle, like the B-24 Fred Betz was on, another gunner lost somewhere in the Marshall Islands overgrowth. Some of the many forever branded Missing in Action.

More than seventy-six thousand American servicemen and servicewomen remain unaccounted for from World War II even now, seventy years later. In addition to Repp, Kukich and Betz, eleven other natives of Medina County are among the unknowns. As most were victims of the air war, it remains unlikely that any trace evidence of their bodies will ever be discovered, let alone identified after all these years. "Missing Forever"—the American tragedy of every war we have chosen to fight.

Next week is Veterans Day, a holiday we actually get close to truly commemorating for what it is. This is not the "Official Beginning of Summer" that we have made out of Memorial Day. It is not an excuse to close public offices to fight midwinter doldrums that evolved out of Presidents' Day. Each November 11 is a time when we appreciate every single one who perceived that service, when it is done in the cause of a nation, is a duty rather than a sacrifice. It is a right and just thing to give honor to every individual who is a veteran. Perhaps it is time that we held them in esteem for more than just twenty-four hours.

They do in Port Clinton, west of here. One of their boys of 1942 found himself in hell, never to return, lost in one of the great war atrocities of the Pacific front. They will not forget that moment in time over there. Bataan Elementary School will remind generations to come of the tragedies and triumphs of the American veteran. By its very name, one school will inspire the study of history so that some day we might finally stop repeating some of our own stupidity.

What a novel idea it would be, not to create a statue so richly deserved but something greater, inspiring another generation. Not naming a building—that would be presumptuous—but rather just a single classroom for one of the Medina servicemen or servicewomen who did so much at one time or another. We do have veterans of every war and conflict this nation has ever waged, save

Another of the stateside beauties—the girl a hero could and would come home to and spend forever with. *Kurjian Family Archives.*

one. The Blanche Sigman Chemistry Lab at Medina. The Horace Messam Library in Wadsworth. The Dick Rowland Theater at Cloverleaf. Perhaps an entire wing of one educational facility to those who never came home and another to the ones who will never be found. Such a simple task, but such a great reward.

The posting of a name almost forgotten might just stimulate almost forgotten concepts. Young people who would see and then inquire. Who would research for answers and discover that education is not what is taught but rather what we all realize in our own time and place. Learning inspired through a simple way to honor our own who believed once and forever that there is no sacrifice when it is duty. Veterans, all veterans of all branches and times, who would rise above the ravages of indifference, never forgotten again.

Then perhaps we could figure out why Veterans Day isn't a school holiday in that place where they did so much, little old Medina County, USA.

SOME INTERESTING QUIRKS FROM WORLD WAR II

When Ferdinand Porsche first started building cars, his chief mechanic was a teenager named Joseph Broz. In later years, Porsche went on to assist in the design of the Panzers for the Third Reich before building his own automobiles after the war. Joseph Broz went on to be Tito and lead Yugoslavia.

At the outbreak of World War II in America, the members of the Japanese diplomatic mission in Washington, D.C., were interred in the five-star resort, the Greenbrier.

During the 1970s, the FBI's idea of investigating the whereabouts of the only German soldier who was still at large after an escape from an American prison camp was to check the phonebooks in large cities to see if he had a telephone number.

As the attack on Pearl Harbor began on December 7, 1941, the last day of a civilian surgeons' convention was just underway in Honolulu.

British intelligence fooled no one when it hired a Montgomery look-alike to thwart assassination attempts on the field marshal's life. Montgomery was vehemently opposed to tobacco use in any form, and his look-alike was a chain smoker.

The company that manufactured Zyklon-B, the poison gas of Nazi extermination camps, always signed its official correspondence, "Always a pleasure to do business with you."

Free French Captain Phillippe de Hautecloque liberated Cameroun in 1940. Four years later, he liberated Paris under the name General LeClerc.

Two stars of the film *The Great Escape*, Donald Pleasance and Hannes Messemer, had both been actual prisoners, Pleasance of the Germans and Messemer of the Russians, during World War II.

Novelist Ernest Hemmingway used his yacht and a Thompson submachine gun to patrol the American coast in search of German U-boats.

German prisoners in Oklahoma required few guards after being shown Hollywood westerns and then told that the Indians lived just over the nearest ridge.

The United States military owned two copies of the top-secret German Enigma encoding machine in the late 1920s.

The first attack on an American warship by the Japanese military was on December 12, 1937. The Imperial Empire apologized for the unfortunate case of mistaken identity even though the ship was flying a forty-foot-long American flag off its stern at the time.

A German weather station was built in Labrador in 1943 and not discovered by the Allies until more than thirty years after the war had ended.

There were actually twelve different women who broadcast under the name "Tokyo Rose" during the course of World War II.

On July 13, 1942, British and German parachutists chose the exact same landing spot for their assault during the Italian campaign.

Shortly after the Normandy invasion, German Field Marshal Erwin Rommel was wounded in an attack by a strafing Allied aircraft. The nearby town he was taken to for treatment was the French village of Montgomery.

Two German prisoners of war held in South Carolina attempted to escape by boarding a local transit bus while still wearing their army uniforms.

Former English King Edward VIII was the intended victim of a German kidnapping plot in Portugal that failed when the Germans rushing to the dock of his ship were involved in an auto accident.

The first two American soldiers into Messina, Sicily, arriving ahead of both Patton and Montgomery, were two sightseeing surgeons from a medical unit still based in North Africa.

A correspondent from the *Chicago Tribune* captured a German platoon during the breakout from the Normandy beachhead in 1944.

During the winter of 1944–45, more than twenty thousand United States servicemen were listed as deserters on their company muster rolls.

The head of German commando operations, Colonel Otto Skorzeny, had to try to surrender four times before he was finally recognized even though he had a unique scar and stood six feet, five inches.

A German submarine survived seven days of almost continual attack as it sailed west before it was finally able to communicate that it had been trying to surrender.

About 80 percent of the Russian male population born in 1923 did not live to see 1946.

About 95 percent of all uniforms, weapons and supplies used by the Allied forces in World War II has been destroyed or scrapped seventy years after the conflict ended.

An entire division of German SS troops once volunteered to fight for the United States in the Pacific against the Japanese. The plan was rejected only after it was determined that the Germans would be entitled to the same benefits as American servicemen and servicewomen after the war.

The *F* in SNAFU does not stand for "fouled."

Adolf Hitler kept a photo of his idol, Henry Ford, on his desk in Berlin, while Henry Ford kept one of Hitler on his desk in Detroit.

The phone number of Hitler's bunker in Berlin was 12-0050. The telephone exchange remained in operation until the last day of the war.

TAKE ME UP THE HILL, SON

Never in the history of mankind has one subject, World War II, inspired such a width and breadth of cinematic stories. From even before the conflict began, filmmakers across the globe were presenting various and assorted perspectives on what would become mankind's most horrific moment. Some were documentary, some were pure fiction and most fell somewhere in between. Fortunately for any student of the conflict today, the overwhelming majority have survived to be appreciated, or ignored, for generations to come.

By no means a definitive list, nor rated by anything but subjectivity on a scale of one to five, these one hundred films are the best (and the worst) the movies have to offer. Just like this text, it's always all about entertainment.

Above Suspicion
Casting Basil Rathbone as a German should be a good indication of the quality of this film. In fact, it says it all. * of 5

All through the Night
It's Bogart in the 1940s—that adds two stars. He's teamed with Conrad Veidt (another star), and the story line is interesting, concerning New York Harbor, but it's not enough for more than an occasional viewing. *** of 5

Anzio
Another offering from 1968 that is best left to Saturday afternoon television on a day where there is absolutely nothing else on. * of 5

Atlantic Convoy
An early war look at the dangers of the Merchant Marine, something Hollywood could understand but the United States government couldn't in 1942. *** of 5

Back to Bataan
If a viewer can get past Anthony Quinn cast as a Filipino, then this John Wayne vehicle is actually very enjoyable. Made in 1945, it has its share of flag-waving propaganda, but there's a liberal share of truth from the conflict as well. **** of 5

Band of Brothers
Even though HBO is not mainstream theater, that point is totally, completely irrelevant for an offering like this. Absolutely one of the top ten films/series of all times in any genre, not the least because of the ability to feel the cold of the Ardennes in 1944. An instant classic. ***** of 5

Bataan
A 1943 purely propaganda film that remains enjoyable to students of the early days of World War II in the South Pacific. **** of 5

Battleground
Another top-ten war film, this James Whitmore/Van Johnson classic in black-and-white should be a required watching for all. ***** of 5

Battle of Britain
An interesting film to viewers who do not need great finishes to their movies. Like the real events, this cinema sputters to a conclusion, relying on the intelligence of the audience to understand the meaning. A good performance by Edward Fox adds a star. *** of 5

Battle of the Bulge
Perhaps the worst treatment of a subject in the history of World War II filmmaking. Absolutely no redeeming value whatsoever. The real problem with this movie is it is three hours too long. 0 of 5

The Best Years of Our Lives
An all-star cast, a perfect sense of timing and an ageless issue treated well combine to make an excellent movie any time. Dealing with the matter of post–World War II posttraumatic stress makes it memorable. ***** of 5

The Big Red One
Lee Marvin should be enough to carry any war film to at least four stars, even at the end of his career, but this is the exception to the rule. It could be worse, but it could have been a lot better. Best watched without commercial interruption. *** of 5

The Bridge at Remagen
Fortunately for this film, there is *The Battle of the Bulge* to keep it from being the worst World War II movie of all time. Short on historical perspective, shorter on script and acting, it is a film well worth missing. 0 of 5

The Bridge Over the River Kwai
It has been more than fifty years since this film hit the screen, winning seven Academy Awards and being declared historically significant. The year 1957 must have been a bad one for movies and historical accuracy. ** of 5

A Bridge Too Far
A mid-1970s offering attempting to make sense of one of the stupidest campaigns in the Allied forces' history of World War II. The campaign fell far short, as does the film in spite of an all-star cast. ** of 5

The Caine Mutiny
Often forgotten as a World War II film because its magnificent cast and tremendous story line make the setting irrelevant. Bogart is incredible, Fred MacMurray really can act and this one should be required watching for all of humanity. ***** of 5

Casablanca
One of the three greatest films ever made in any genre, so brilliantly scripted and so masterfully acted that the world to this day has yet to realize that it was December 6, 1941, when Ilsa first walks into Rick's Café Américain. ***** of 5

The Colditz Story
Another 1950s film that takes real life to make an entertaining movie. The real history of Colditz is captured like a POW, the cast is good and the result is well worth seeing…or seeing again. **** of 5

Confessions of a Nazi Spy
Purely propaganda and purely prewar, but still enjoyable, if for no other reason than the casting of Edward G. Robinson and George Sanders in the same film. **** of 5

Corregidor
A totally forgettable cast, script and message leaves this attempt at propaganda far behind even for a Saturday afternoon. * of 5

Cross of Iron
An interesting movie casting James Coburn into the German army on the Russian front, surviving battle as much as his own cynicism along the way. Not as masterful as *Das Boot* by any stretch of the imagination, but the effort to show another side has its moments. *** of 5

The Dam Busters
From a book by the same author who penned *The Great Escape*, this is a film most of the baby boomers had for a first World War II experience, and a good experience it was. Well researched and well acted, it deserves much more play than received in recent years. **** of 5

Das Boot
Another of the greatest war films ever produced, but please, pronounce it *boat* and not *boot*. Brilliantly acted and superbly filmed, and the script can make any loyal, red-blooded American root for the enemy. Absolutely superb. ***** of 5

The Desert Fox
German Field Marshal Erwin Rommel with an English accent makes for a most unique approach to docu-drama film. Another Saturday afternoon nothing-to-do time filler. ** of 5

The Desert Rats
An interesting premise that could well have been a good movie, but it isn't. It's not much more than another Saturday afternoon filler. ** of 5

Destination Tokyo
Cary Grant at his finest, a mid-war propaganda/feel good movie below the waves, and it works on every facet. A nice two hours spent. **** of 5

The Devil's Brigade
The story is based on real events and the cast is good, and yet this one seems to fall short of everything except improving Canadian-U.S. relationships. ** of 5

The Diary of Anne Frank
The required high school reading for most American students, this 1959 movie is a very good presentation of the terror those about to face the Holocaust must have endured. A classic performance by Shelly Winters moves the film from most average to worth watching. *** of 5

The Dirty Dozen
A total fiction that made one of the great World War II films of all time. Great casting, superb scripting and a certain appeal to the villain in all of us. ***** of 5

The Eagle Has Landed
A movie that tends to bore, perhaps as much because of scripting as Robert Duval and Donald Sutherland sleepwalking through their roles. A "no reason to watch" film. ** of 5

The Enemy Below
If there hadn't been *Das Boot*, this would be the greatest submarine movie in the history of warfare. Curt Jurgens is incredible, the plot is totally believable and it has an outstanding offering of both sides of the story. ***** of 5

The Fighting Seabees
It's John Wayne, it's made in the middle of the war and it's pure propaganda/feel patriotic/cheer for the noble guys. A totally average, totally predicable film. ** of 5

The Fighting Sullivans
Yet another filmed mid-war biopic that relives and dies with one family's tragedy at Guadalcanal. Not a great cast, not a great script and not a great watch. ** of 5

Flags of Our Fathers
There were great expectations for this film, a Clint Eastwood production, a subject matter that inspires every American, and it fails miserably in almost every aspect. ** of 5

Flying Fortress
An early war release starring the man who would become television's Robin Hood, this film has action and plot, but sadly it has nothing worth seeing the second time. ** of 5

Flying Leathernecks
A "John Wayne will win the war" classic, it's well worth watching seventy years later. **** of 5

Flying Tigers
Released about the same time as *Flying Fortress*, this is another John Wayne vehicle guaranteeing American victory created strictly as a matter of morale. All the same, a good watch now and then. *** of 5

Force 10 from Navarone
Filmed without a shred of historical accuracy, simply a low-quality sequel to *Guns of Navarone*, it still is an extremely entertaining movie. Robert Shaw and Edward Fox more than offset a wooden Harrison Ford, well worth enjoying especially to any unfamiliar with the difference between Partisan and Chetnik. **** of 5

Foreign Correspondent
A 1940 film that is nearly as entertaining as *Kelly's Heroes*. Joel McCrea and George Sanders combine with a decent script for one worth seeing and then seeing again. **** of 5

Four Jills and a Jeep
Entertainment is the theme, and the end result in one of the very few films to highlight the great people of the USO. Nicely done from start to finish. **** of 5

Frogmen
An early 1950s film short on propaganda or flag waving, long on details of a most forgotten side of the military in World War II. *** of 5

From Here to Eternity
Eight Academy Awards were presented for work on this film. As a drama at the time, perhaps it earned them, as the cast is magnificent. As a war film, it's generous to give it three stars, so I won't. ** of 5

God Is My Co-Pilot
This does what *Flying Tigers* should have. It is a great look at the real life and times of that theater. Nicely done and a good watch, especially without commercial interruption. **** of 5

The Great Dictator
If you like Charlie Chaplin, then you will enjoy this attempt at ridiculing of Hitler. If you don't, you'll find another film. * of 5

The Great Escape
Yes, there are a few historical inaccuracies. Yes, it is one of the top five World War II films of all time. Superb acting, scripting and the most haunting theme music ever composed. ***** of 5

Guadalcanal Diary
Anthony Quinn transfers to the South Pacific and becomes Filipino, but that isn't enough to discourage watching a really good, if not great, look at Guadalcanal. **** of 5

The Guns of Navarone
An enjoyable fiction with the ever-flexible Anthony Quinn playing a marvelous foil to Gregory Peck. Why it was necessary to add James Darren to the film is the true mystery, but it is enjoyable for David Niven's antics all the same. *** of 5

Halls of Montezuma
A Marine biopic set in World War II South Pacific, it sets a standard of subsequent offerings throughout the 1950s. Not great but not terrible, it is more Saturday afternoon television fare. *** of 5

Hangmen Also Die
The subject is fascinating, the script is terrible and the acting totally forgettable. Nowhere near a classic—perhaps it was a little better when it comes to accuracy. * of 5

Hitler: The Last Ten Days
The producers, writers and actors should thank God that there is a film called *Battle of the Bulge*. That is the only reason this is not the worst war film of all time. 0 of 5

In Harm's Way
In spite of Otto Preminger's involvement, it's the ultimate yawner of World War II films. Not worth the time. 0 of 5

Is Paris Burning?
No, but they should have burned this script, film and every paycheck associated with it. 0 of 5

Judgment at Nuremberg
It takes a great deal to out-act Spencer Tracey, but Maximilian Schell does just that in this 1961 docu-drama classic. Set in the aftermath of the war, it is stunning in black-and-white, but even more so for the thought-provoking script. **** of 5

Kelly's Heroes
Made for the baby boomer generation, this film has a total implausibility factor that is totally ignored. Simply one of the most enjoyable war films ever made, baby. ***** of 5

King Rat
James Clavell lived it, and then he wrote about it, and the story truly comes through in a very forgotten side of the war, concering Japanese abuses in POW camps of Asia. **** of 5

Letters from Iwo Jima
If you must watch, watch the English dubbed version. Even at that, you too may wonder why or how this one won an Academy Award. * of 5

The Life and Death of Colonel Blimp
An English homefront narrative that amuses in the name of history. An enjoyable rainy day film, not a classic, but it's entertaining if anybody can understand English humor. *** of 5

The Longest Day
An early 1960s epic that does succeed even in black-and-white in spite of John Wayne's acting. At least the English bulldog is magnificent, and it is a tremendous film, even if the world does not remember the last line. ***** of 5

Marine Raiders
A talented cast and the story surrounding Guadalcanal should be interesting, but the script destroys any reason to bother with it. * of 5

Memphis Belle
Perhaps the biggest sleeper of all World War II movies. A cast that is believable, a historically accurate script and good all-around flow of action throughout. A very nice film too often unjustly overlooked. ***** of 5

Merrill's Marauders
The young guns of 1962 Hollywood join together and re-create one of the greatest combat units of the South Pacific war. An excellent treatment of a unit that defied the odds from beginning to end. **** of 5

Midway
An attempt at an epic version of an interesting subject, an all-star cast and some of the worst cinematography in the history of filmmaking conspire to make this a film not much better than Charlton Heston's attempt at acting. ** of 5

Mosquito Squadron
A British-made "love in war between battles" story that can be interesting and incredibly bland in the same ninety minutes. David McCallum gives it an extra star. *** of 5

Mrs. Miniver
An early war drama that mingles the terror of the Blitz with English family values. Greer Garson is fine, Walter Pidgeon is predictable and some call it a classic. Not all though. *** of 5

Objective, Burma!
Errol Flynn goes to war and does it well in this late-war production. Strictly a vehicle for the star, it does manage to entertain. **** of 5

Operation Pacific
Another "John Wayne wins the war" feature, this time in the South Pacific. Predictable from opening credits to finish, even with Patricia Neal. ** of 5

Operation Petticoat
Light comedy, totally and completely unrelated to anything historical other than being set in World War II. Amusing entertainment and nothing more. ** of 5

Patton
The theme music alone would rate four stars. Coupled with the cast, the historic accuracy and the script, it is now and always will be a definitive war movie. ***** of 5

Pearl Harbor
Hollywood pretty boys take on World War II and win it single-handedly. One of the dozen or so films of the subject not worth watching more than once. * of 5

PT-109
If JFK hadn't been elected president of the United States, they never would have made this film. They shouldn't have anyway. 0 of 5

Run Silent, Run Deep
A very good book led to a different but equally good script. Joined by actors who are as believable in character as they are talented, and a classic is born and survives forever. ***** of 5

Sahara
Jim Belushi makes another attempt at acting in a film that has a script, cast and direction about as colorful as the movie's desert setting. ** of 5

Sands of Iwo Jima
Perhaps not the greatest war movie of all times, but it is certainly the best Pacific Theater offering ever made. A perfect blend of Hollywood and documentary film, even if John Wayne finally dies on film. ***** of 5

Saving Private Ryan
It's not *Band of Brothers*, but it certainly is close. DreamWorks Pictures and Paramount Pictures got it right, from script to cast to performance. ***** of 5

Schindler's List
A film that received seven Academy Awards and was hailed as one of the greatest movies of all time by the American Film Institute; it is a marvelous

indication that politically correct filmmaking doesn't mean good, let alone great. ** of 5

The Sea Wolves
A 1980 rarely seen film featuring Gregory Peck and based somewhat in historical fact. An underwhelming effort on all fronts, not to be confused with *The Sea Wolf*. ** of 5

Sherlock Holmes and the Secret Weapon
The greatest fictional detective of all time is transported to win World War II. Actually, it's a fairly good film only because it's Basil and Nigel. *** of 5

Sherlock Holmes and the Voice of Terror
See entry above. *** of 5

Sink the Bismarck!
An English movie with an English point of view, this is a well-done treatment of the story as well as the fact that Hollywood did not win the war after all. **** of 5

Ski Patrol
Another prewar American production that has no purpose other than to show off winter sports and bad scripts. * of 5

So Proudly We Hail
One of the great World War II films, even more so for treating the subject of Pacific nurses under fire that is often overlooked. Outstanding script and acting. ***** of 5

South of the Border
A prewar American-made film that couples Old Mexico, Nazism and a generous dose of flag waving to absolutely no effect. * of 5

Stalag 17
One of the three greatest movies ever made, but only if the dark side of humanity and a noticeable lack of heroes is acceptable to the viewer. Perhaps there is a little bit of Joey in all of us, even as we pray that there isn't. ***** of 5

The Story of G.I. Joe
One of the ten best World War II films ever made, even though the real-life conclusion was one of the war's greatest tragedies. Robert Mitchum does nothing for the film, and Burgess Meredith does everything in a do-not-miss classic. ***** of 5

They Were Expendable
John Wayne does not win the war, but he ensures that America will in this fairly good look at some of the most courageous sailors in history, the PT boat crews. **** of 5

13 Rue Madeleine
A totally predictable film but still entertaining given the excellent work of Richard Conti. Cagney is good and the script is average, but it was 1947 too. *** of 5

Thirty Seconds Over Tokyo
The Doolittle Raid is portrayed here at its finest, taken from a great book written by an actual participant of the action. The script is good, the film work is outstanding and the acting is excellent. A classic of the highest order. ***** of 5

To Have and Have Not
Another of the greatest three films ever made, World War II is actually a subplot to the greatest love story in the history of Hollywood. It's Bogart and Bacall, and that is all that matters. ***** of 5

Tora! Tora! Tora!
Whether it's the poor film quality, the mediocre script or the waste of acting talent, this treatment of Pearl Harbor isn't the worst…but it's far from the best. ** of 5

Train
John Frankenheimer usually can turn out a classic with a decent script and adequate actors. Unfortunately, even he can't really save this one from mediocrity. *** of 5

12 o'Clock High
Another of the definitive war films, especially for a liberal use of actual combat footage. If a viewer can stand life's ultimate tragedy, the dog dying, it is a do-not-miss movie. ***** of 5

U-571
Totally historically incorrect, and yet the film is fairly good, entertaining and well acted on many levels. Certainly not the best submarine movie of all time, but it's worth watching now and then. *** of 5

Valkyrie
If what Tom Cruise does matters, this is a film to see…once. For the rest of the world, it is far better to watch the History Channel treatments of the same subject. * of 5

Von Ryan's Express
More often than not, Frank Sinatra just does not work well as a World War II figure, no matter the role. This is a "more often" entry, a most average effort and script. ** of 5

Wake Island
Filmed within weeks of the battle itself, this is pure propaganda, but it's still somewhat entertaining, much more so than big-budget productions of twenty years later. *** of 5

The War Lover
Steve McQueen as a B-17 pilot in an English production start to finish does not really sound like a classic. It certainly gets close, though—well worth a watch. **** of 5

Where Eagles Dare
Despite a screenplay by Alistair McLean and a cast including Richard Burton and Clint Eastwood, a most average, underwhelming film from 1968. ** of 5

The White Cliffs of Dover
A "two wars on the homefront" film made during the earliest days of World War II and without the benefit of hindsight. Good for a drama, poor for a war film. The script, cast and acting all fall just short of the middle. ** of 5

Windtalkers
A tremendous subject shabbily treated. The Code Talkers deserved much more than this. * of 5

The Young Lions
Odd choices in casting and an uneven script ensure that no matter how well regarded an actor might be, there is much more to greatness than this film not really worth seeing. ** of 5

INDEX

ABOUT THE AUTHOR

E li Beachy is a newspaper columnist with the *Medina County Gazette*, as well as the obedient servant to one loving wife and five demanding cats.